Radiance!

Radiance!

Breathwork, Movement & Body-Centered Psychotherapy

Gay Hendricks, Ph.D. &
Kathlyn Hendricks, Ph.D., ADTR

Wingbow Press
Berkeley, California

Printed in the United States of America.

Originally published as *At the Speed of Love* by The Hendricks Institute Publishing Company, Colorado Springs, Colorado.

Cover and book design by Paula Morrison.
Typeset by Campaigne and Associates Typography.

ISBN 0-914728-72-5

Wingbow Books are published and distributed by Bookpeople, 2929 Fifth Street, Berkeley, California 94710.

First Wingbow edition: March, 1991.

WARNING! Breathwork, movement therapy and body-oriented psychotherapy are complex subjects. This book is designed for educational purposes, not as a substitute for training or psychotherapy. None of the techniques mentioned in this book should be embarked upon without formal training. Those seeking training in the techniques should correspond with us at The Hendricks Institute, P.O. Box 994, Colorado Springs, CO 80901. A list of certified practitioners is also available from the above address. The terms Radiance Breathwork, Radiance Movement Therapy, Radiance Prenatal Process and The Hendricks Method of Body-Oriented Psychotherapy are registered by The Hendricks Institute and may not be used without permission.

Table of Contents

Preface:
Love, Technique and Integrity: The Healing Tripod 1

Chapter 1:
How Deep Transformation Works: Introducing Our Method 3

Chapter 2:
How to Do Radiance Breathwork With Individuals 13

Chapter 3:
Leading Radiance Group Breathwork. 37

Chapter 4:
Techniques For Clearing Birth, Prenatal and Conception Issues 43

Chapter 5:
Radiance Movement Therapy 51

Chapter 6:
The Bodymind Centering Techniques 67

Chapter 7:
On Getting What You Want: Our Method of Manifestation. 81

Chapter 8:
Energy Centers of the Body. 101

Chapter 9:
Frequently Asked Questions 111

Chapter 10:
Aphorisms and Notes on Therapy and Transformation 119

Appendix 125

Love, Technique and Integrity: The Healing Tripod

Ours is a time of rapidly expanding possibilities for transformation. A few hundred years ago only scant options existed for the person who sought healing: prayer, potions, a visit to a sacred place, exorcism. All of these required that the person be demonstrably sick. Now thousands of techniques abound, and we do not even have to be "sick" in order to get better. With such a dizzying array to choose from, how is the student to decide what to study? How is the prospective client to know whether a given approach or practitioner will empty the ego, or simply the wallet?

A distinguishing feature of our method is that it rests on a tripod of three elements, each of which is crucial, but when combined together produces reliable results. The three elements of the tripod are love, technique and integrity. The techniques we use are extremely powerful and have been distilled through two decades of experience. Anyone who has witnessed one of our breathwork or movement therapy sessions will agree that they have been present at a deeply moving event. But technique, no matter how artfully applied, can never be truly useful unless it comes from a context of love. There are teachers, many in number, who have invented or transmitted many powerful techniques, but the context in which they are delivered is tainted with manipulation, power hunger, scarcity or greed. We feel very strongly that the only healing context can be love, both the tender and the tough. Tender love embraces all; tough love can set boundaries and limits. Both are equally important, and we as practitioners must be actively engaged in giving tough and tender love to ourselves so that we can love our clients effectively.

Integrity is the third element of the tripod. There are plenty of teachers nowadays who have powerful techniques and even a loving presence, but who have little integrity. One of the most pathetic and disturbing images of our time is the TV evangelist who is caught cruising the back streets in a wig looking for someone to play out the pornographic fantasies he decries on Sunday. It would take pages to list all the therapists, teachers and gurus who have fallen due to sexual or financial violations. One definition of integrity, then, relates to sound moral principle: If we seek help, we have every right to expect that we will not be violated or misled by those whom we trust to heal us. But another definition of integrity is "a state of completion or wholeness." We have a right to demand of our healers that they walk their talk. This is an era when we have raised the requirements of our leaders. We no longer will settle, for example, for learning about meditation from a teacher. We want a teacher whose life *is* meditation. These are tough demands, but then these are tough times and require a kind of absoluteness that might not have been necessary a short while ago.

What is obvious now is that the stakes are high. We must heal ourselves while healing the planet. Our relationships, between individuals and between nations, must transcend conflict or be blown apart by enormous forces. This is the background against which we have developed our Method, over twenty years of work with some of the most courageous people we can imagine. By being with people as they healed their bodies and their relationships, then reached up into the outer regions of higher consciousness, we have come to have an unshakable confidence in the power of human beings to live in a state of positive energy.

If this is your goal, we congratulate you and welcome you to our book.

CHAPTER ONE

How Deep Transformation Works: Introducing Our Method

If you cannot find it in your own body, you will not find it elsewhere.
—The Upanishads

The Healing Journey Is Into the Body, Not Out of It

*I*n our years as body-oriented psychotherapists, we have been privileged to be with thousands of courageous people as they have journeyed through deep and life-changing transformations. Although these changes have been infinitely and intricately different, they have had one element in common: They were accomplished by journeying into the body, not out of it. Each person tuned in to his or her bodily experience, amplified it through breath and movement, and flowed with the emerging waves of energy. The results have often been miraculous, and always wondrous to behold.

The Main Healing Agents Are Truth and Love

*O*ur window to these vistas is a form of body-oriented psychotherapy we have developed over the past two decades. The tools are exquisitely primal: breath, movement, touch, awareness. Beyond these techniques, the main healing agents are truth and love. Applied in an artful manner, these simple and profound techniques bring forth experiences from the depths, the heights, even the dawn of humankind. The method promotes rapid change, because the pillars of the process are truth and love, which are beyond time and therefore do not take time. We invite people to open up to the truth of what they are experiencing, and to tell the truth in fine detail. We love them for what they are experiencing, and invite them to love themselves. Truth and love act as catalysts in hastening us all to our full evolution. In fact, they are such rapid catalysts that many people find that a little bit of truth and love begins to change everything in their lives. When the change begins, and the old world based on lies and pain starts to crumble, many people become scared and pull back from the truth. They attempt to close the door again, but it will not be easily shut. This is why we ask people if they are willing to go all the way. They all need to know that there will often be a period of things falling apart before a new life emerges that is coherent and based on truth and love.

Two Clinical Examples

*L*ook with us at two specific examples. A woman, 33, described a "squirrelly" place at the base of her sternum. As she described it, her face grimaced with distaste. We asked her to explore the feeling through movement. She tuned in to the squirrelly feeling, and began to move with the feeling. A pattern to her movement emerged. She dashed furiously across the room, then collapsed. The collapse had a "give-up" quality to it. Kathlyn asked her to go further into the give-up place. She did, and described it as beige in color. Encouraged to go further, she began to writhe on the floor, sobbing and saying, "I can't get out." The intensity of the moment subsided, and she realized her whole life pattern was tied to this cycle of rushing furiously, then collapsing. It became clear to her that the pattern came from the style of her own birth. Further exploration revealed that her birth was difficult, with much anesthesia used in the final stages. A drama of birth was revealed, within minutes, by focusing consciousness on a squirrelly feeling in the chest.

Another example: Two successful professionals came in to work on their relationship. Their complaint was vague. Things had not been going well, and after several years together they felt stuck. They rarely got close, and when they did, a conflict often ensued. The current cycle of conflict began when he said he wanted to move to a higher level of intimacy.

We invited them to tune in to how they were feeling in their bodies right then. They felt drained, with low energy. We asked them to go further into those feelings, to put all their awareness into the feelings of low energy and being drained. She yawned—his jaw clenched slightly—their bodies swayed. We invited them to come closer to each other. She looked like she was about to fall asleep; he looked angry and scared.

"Don't fight it," we said. "Let yourself yawn more." She did, and looked as if she would pass out. We steered her to a couch and invited her to surrender to what she was feeling. "My jaws are so tense," she said. We massaged her jaws as she opened wide. A strong smell of anesthesia pervaded the room. She began to talk rapidly about being in the dentist's chair when she was 12. She was being gassed and wouldn't go under. The dentist was angry; she was terrified; and there was something sexually arousing about it. (The nitrous oxide was probably liberating some of her newly-awakening sexual feelings.) She was hallucinating about relatives being taken to the gas chamber. "Open wide, open wide," the dentist was shouting. And she sobbed.

The pattern had emerged. Her partner's demands for intimacy had triggered one of her life's most horrible memories. More demands for closeness (Open! Open wide!) and more sexual feelings meant violation and terror and sleepiness. All these things had been just below her awareness. No wonder she felt drained; all her energy had gone into fighting off these ancient wolves from her unconscious.

His pattern fit hers snugly. He was replaying a drama from his relationship with his mother. The more he wanted closeness, the further she would withdraw, until finally he would lash out in anger. So, of course, out of 2.5 billion women on earth, he got into a relationship with one who literally got numb and sleepy when he demanded closeness.

How does one move from two people complaining of a lack of closeness to having one of them lying on the couch in the grip of a decades-old trauma? And within five minutes? The technique is simple; prepare, however, to spend a lifetime mastering it. The therapist and the client must focus awareness on the body and its sensations, amplify these sensations through breath and movement, and continue following them as patterns emerge. The direction is always deeper and further, until an organic resolution is reached.

Part of the art is to let movement and breath turn into metaphor. His arms look "held back." Her breathing is "labored." Her upper body looks as if it is trying to "get away" from her lower body. His shoulders look "burdened." Not every metaphor will resonate. Eventually, if you are observant, humble and sufficiently lucky, a connection will happen. The person will shift to a deeper level of awareness and something authentic will emerge. In a first session with a middle-aged woman, we listened to her story of why she wanted to work on herself. But while the words poured out, her breathing was telling a deeper truth. Her belly was tight, forcing all her breath up into her chest. Her breathing was about twice the speed it should normally have been, and the shallow pumping of her chest had a labored quality to it. Her shoulders slumped; she looked burdened from above and girdled from below. Not surprisingly, she spoke of anxiety and depression, which had been her constant companions for several years. We pointed out the effortful quality of her breath and the rock-solid, held-in quality of her stomach. She had not been aware of either of these indisputable realities of her body, but when she noticed them her breathing deepened. Actually, she let down her guard for a moment and took one deep breath into her belly. Her tears came with a rush, and she sobbed for many minutes, while we encouraged her to stay with her sadness and to continue breathing through it. After a while she felt much better, but we chose not to stop there. With our support, she let herself keep breathing, now with a deeper and more relaxed belly-breath. Soon her face replaced its sallow gray with a pink glow. A smile began on her face, at first tentatively and then more broadly. She was discovering the organic positive feelings that are our reward when we let ourselves participate fully with long held-back emotion.

What emerges when people breathe and move and focus consciousness on themselves? It is typical to feel everything from long-held emotions, such as grief and rage, to birth trauma, even to exalted spiritual awareness. Sometimes all of these phenomena emerge in a single session. It is common to begin with a simple movement such as picking a thumbnail and find that it is connected to a personality issue (such as fear of a parent's disapproval). When this theme is explored to its source, it is often connected to being unwanted at—or before—birth. When the birth and prenatal feelings are experienced deeply, a spiritual realization may emerge, such as "I'm free and divine; I can be a source of approval for myself and others."

What We Have Learned

*T*hese remarkable journeys have taught us more than we ever imagined we could know, and yet we still feel that we are only at the beginning of possibilities. Here are some of our learnings so far.

PEOPLE ARE FUNDAMENTALLY GOOD, AND PEOPLE ARE FUNDAMENTALLY GOD

Beneath all the family and societal conditioning, people are clear, straightforward and happy. At the deepest level, people are connected to the divine element of the universe. By opening up to the deepest levels of themselves, people uncover their organic clarity, happiness and divinity. Nothing needs to be added. We are already what we seek.

A related finding is: What is within can be trusted. The unconscious is not to be feared or resisted. It simply contains what we could not handle at a prior time. Resisting it makes it seem dangerous and mean. As Jesus is reported to have said, "If you bring forth what is within you, what is within you will save you. If you do not bring forth what is within you, what is within you will destroy you."

THE BODY IS SACRED

Many well-intentioned therapists still feel that the body is somehow less holy than the mind or the spirit. This attitude, due no doubt to unexplored territory in their own bodies, limits their effectiveness as therapists. We have found that mind, body and spirit are all one, all sacred. We have worked with many psychics, meditators and gurus who have problems in their lives precisely because they have made a split in themselves between mind and spirit, sexuality and spirituality, heaven and earth.

People often mention that they experience stronger feelings of transcendence after a session of body therapy than during meditation. Meditation is a wonderful tool, which we have both used daily for years, and it seems to work even better when combined with practices which honor the body and its energy. Spirituality is best achieved through a process of embracing all. The old myth of spirituality says that holiness is attained through denial and limiting awareness: the priest shuns marriage, the yogi sits in a cave. But now a new possibility is open, for spirituality to saturate all areas of our lives. Any separation, any area we fail to embrace, shows up in our lives as trouble.

ANSWERS ACTUALLY DO LIE WITHIN

Someone said that prayer is talking to God, while meditation is listening. We are used to talking to our bodies, and then to telling our bodies what to do, but less skilled at listening to them. An outcome of our method of therapy is that the person comes to listen to the body's wisdom. Am I really hungry, or is it because I just saw that pizza commercial on TV? Are my shoulders tense because I'm angry, or scared, or both? Do these stomach quivers mean I'm in love or in fear?

Even with our courageous and willing clients, much work is needed to help them learn to listen to their bodies. Society teaches people not to listen to their inner selves. If you are not feeling well, take a pill. If you are lonely, light a cigarette and have a glass of wine. If you want to be different, buy something. When people wake up from this societal trance and learn to listen to their own bodies' signals, their lives change profoundly.

THE BODY CONTAINS MULTITUDES

As Walt Whitman said, "I am large, I contain multitudes." It continually inspires us that the body remembers so much. Imprinted in the muscles, cells and in mysterious processes yet to be decoded are memories of the cataclysms of birth, spine-shuddering fears, transcendent joy, and rages of the crib. All this can be accessed through the healing power of truth and love. Mystics have been telling us for centuries that God is visible in a grain of sand, as the oak tree is already in the acorn. So it is with the body.

The agony, as well as the divinity, is already latent in the arch of an eyebrow or a hitch in the breath. Called forth skillfully, symptoms and glitches can be our most efficient pathways to the wonders of creation. What is there is exactly what needs to be loved. As people work on themselves through our methods of movement and breathing, they go through distinctive layers of psychospiritual issues. In a single session, clients may move through issues from childhood, then go down into birth struggles and even conception. They may move finally into the transpersonal realm, directly connecting with bliss, love and oneness. Diagrammed, the trend of the work proceeds from the outer, more visible layers down into the mystic depths.

Willingness

*W*illingness is a safe and gentle way of going beyond the ego. In order for change to take place, people must go beyond what is known. New possibilities emerge in the open space when people can let go of what they think are the possibilities.

For example, a woman in a therapy group was unable to find a job. Trained in a highly specialized field, she claimed that she had interviewed at every one of the several firms that employed her specialty. We asked her if she would be willing for a job to emerge. She replied with a litany of "Yes, buts . . ." Among these were, "Yes, but I've tried everything," "Yes, but there's a recession on," and "Yes, but I don't want to move to a new city." When she had exhausted these (which we sometimes call getting off your "but"), we asked again if she would be willing to have a job emerge. Finally she gave us a straight yes, although she had no idea how this might come about. The next week she reported that a company, where she had been turned down previously, had called and asked if she were still available. It seems they had just received a new contract and urgently needed her specialty.

The ego is the great pretender. It pretends to know the best way to go about things; it pretends to have all the answers. This is understandable, because everything it has always done has worked: You're still alive, aren't you? Since it is the repository of what has kept you alive in the past, it is afraid to jump off into the unknown— to stand in the void of "I don't know" and wait for a creative new pattern to emerge.

Willingness dispenses with the limitations of time and space. If you are unwilling to face a fear of elevators, for example, you must go linearly through time, creating one elevator after another until you can face the fear. The moment you become willing to deal with the fear, you no longer need to create future experiences of it. Space no longer is an issue, either. If you become willing to experience your fear of elevators, it doesn't matter that the nearest one is miles away.

Willingness gently collapses time and space. One Sunday afternoon, Gay had an awareness of an issue he needed to clear up with his daughter, then 2,000

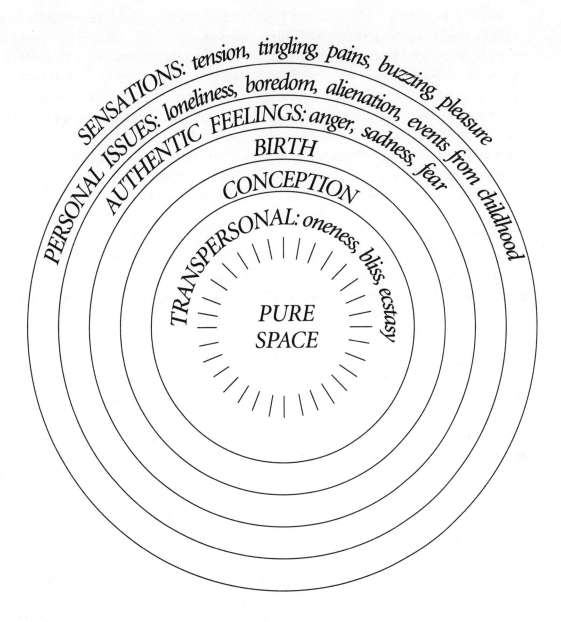

SENSATIONS: tension, tingling, pains, buzzing pleasure

PERSONAL ISSUES: loneliness, boredom, alienation, events from childhood

AUTHENTIC FEELINGS: anger, sadness, fear

BIRTH

CONCEPTION

TRANSPERSONAL: oneness, bliss, ecstasy

PURE SPACE

Layers of the Self
Revealed
in Deep Energy Work

miles away at school. A few minutes later the phone rang, and his daughter said, "What's up?" She had suddenly felt the urge to call.

There are several willingnesses that can make life, and therapy, much easier. One is the willingness to take each experience as it comes. A great deal of human energy is needlessly expended in resisting the present experience. "Is this the experience I ought to be having?" is a poor use of the mind. Duality is created through this style of thinking. For example, a couple in counseling spent several sessions uncovering what was bothering them. When it came down to the core issue, it was that both of them had sexual feelings they feared discussing. It was out of bounds in their relationship to admit sexual feelings, even if, in this case, many of the feelings were toward Tom Cruise and Jessica Lange. "If you have sexual feelings for anyone else, then it means you don't love me; and if you don't love me I'm lost because I've become so dependent on you." So, a great amount of energy had to be expended in keeping sexual feelings out of awareness and in lying to each other about the issue. Naturally, human beings are the direct result of millions of years of sexy ancestors, so we will have sexual feelings around a lamppost if we stay near it for a while. When this couple stopped pretending that they weren't having the experiences they were having, their problems smoothed out.

The willingness to express the truth is a watershed moment in life. There are many barriers to expressing the truth, not the least of which are the painful consequences of having done so as children. In society at large, it was only a short while ago that Galileo was threatened with burning at the stake for saying the earth orbited the sun. On a more intimate scale, both of the authors can recall being punished as children for uttering truths which the family had tacitly agreed to repress.

When clients tell us their lives are not working, we begin to look for where they are not telling the truth. One client came in after the holidays feeling very depressed. We asked her to increase her slump in the chair and to amplify her sighing and averted gaze. She began to uncover a long list of untruths: things she had needed but had not asked for, confrontations she had placated, internal messages she had ignored, and things she felt enraged about (such as a spouse's obnoxious drunken behavior) that she had swallowed to keep the peace. Her depression began to make sense, and to lift, as she sorted through the numerous times she had not told the truth.

Two other keys are the willingness to take responsibility for one's life and the willingness to judge one's true motivations by looking at the results one has created. Taking responsibility means dropping projection, the tendency to blame anyone or anything for the circumstances and events of life. It involves asking, without rancor, the question: What am I doing to create this reality? This question is especially important when we are most convinced that it actually is the other person's fault, that there is no possible way we could have anything to do with it. In the example of the couple who had difficulty with sexual feelings, the wife was absolutely convinced it was her husband's problem. He was the one who had these sexual feelings for other women, including Jessica Lange, whom the wife thought to be disgustingly unattractive. A breakthrough occurred when she realized that she, too, had sexual feelings for others, including Tom Cruise, whom her husband considered a "real greaser." When she was willing to drop projection and take responsibility for her own feelings, the problem became solvable.

Judging our true motivations from the results we create sidesteps the ego. If, for example, you consciously intend to be in a close relationship, while the observable reality is that you are not, you could feed your ego by attributing the reasons to the widely-known deficiencies of the opposite sex. But you could also look at the results you are creating and determine that perhaps you have an unconscious intention that overrides the conscious one. A client once said, "I want a close relationship but no one has come along." We explored whether she might have unconscious intentions that were getting in the way. Ultimately, she began to take responsibility for what she was creating. She became aware that she was avoiding a relationship in which she could clear up a fear of being alone and unworthy. Once she became aware of these issues, she changed her statement to, "I want a close relationship and I am choosing to be alone right now." Very quickly, a new relationship emerged.

Willingness often seems to work like magic. Recently in a workshop, a woman came in late and looking very rattled. She said she had lost her pack containing all her money, documents and personal possessions somewhere in the city. Since we were discussing willingness in the workshop at the time, we asked her if we could use her pack as an example. She agreed, and we asked her if she would quit worrying about it and let it reappear "as if by magic." After some discourse she agreed. The next day she reported with elation that she had gone home to find her pack, possessions intact, hanging on her doorknob. A kind stranger had found it and driven it to her house.

The Ultimate Learning

*A*s therapists, we often come to the place where we do not know what will happen next. At this magic moment when the ego recedes, we rely on love and consciousness. We ask the person to return awareness to the body and its sensations, or we simply love them as much as we can. Miracles unfold from this moment. A tense neck lets go; emotions pour forth; pain turns to ecstasy. The moment never occurs if we are looking for it or trying to make it happen. It only happens when we remember to go beyond what we know and trust the healing power of the universe itself.

Problems begin when consciousness is withdrawn from some part of ourselves. When consciousness is withdrawn, energy also withdraws. In the stagnant place left behind, illness occurs. For example, nuns have an abnormally high rate of breast and uterine cancer. This may be because they are withdrawing consciousness from these areas, thus reducing the flow of life energy through the areas. When we can help a person get energy and consciousness back into an area of the body, symptoms disappear.

Countless times we have been with people as they have experienced pain, and have chosen to open up to it rather than continue to hide it. As a result of being willing to feel their pain, they awakened more energy and joy than they had before. As a species, we would be wise to follow this path. As human beings we must get beneath our superficial differences, open up to our collective fear and pain, and recover the natural joy and respect for life that is our birthright. If we resist our divinity, projecting the light outside rather than opening up to our own inner light, we may force the all-consuming nuclear flash that will vaporize all flesh and hope.

Facing the pain and awakening to love and light are not only the best choice—at this stage of evolution they are the only choice.

CHAPTER TWO

How to Do Radiance Breathwork with Individuals

The smoke of my own breath, echoes, ripples . . . I sing the body electric.
—Walt Whitman

We have found breathwork to be one of the most powerful catalysts of transformation available in this era. In this chapter I (GH) will describe how we developed the process, how I have used it in my own evolution, and how to use it with clients. The breathwork we have developed comes in two general forms: cathartic and centering. Almost every client needs to learn how to use breath to feel more centered. Later in the chapter you will find the techniques I use for this purpose. Some clients need a deeper form of breathwork to release them from the grip of old emotional patterns or trauma from early developmental stages such as conception or birth. For these situations cathartic breathwork was developed. This form of breathwork differs from rebirthing, Reichian therapy or any other form currently taught. We call it Radiance Breathwork because our clients frequently use the term "radiant" when we ask them how they feel after a session. It can assist in the transformation process in several ways:

1. Breathwork releases unresolved emotions held in the body. As I tell my clients: "Whatever you can breathe through loses its grip on you." Typically, people flush out recent feelings when they first start breathing, then progress backward through time. Often a recent feeling is actually rooted in an issue that began at birth or even conception.

2. Breathwork increases the amount of positive energy a person can handle. The body has a psychological thermostat on how much energy it will let itself feel. Breathwork readjusts the thermostat slightly upwards each time it is done properly.

3. Breathwork allows the person to focus on, and ultimately master, the problem of resistance to positive energy, which can be considered the fundamental psycho-spiritual problem. Resistance, which may be elusive elsewhere, is readily apparent in the hitches, glitches and hesitancies of each breath. Breath is therefore the perfect place to focus on resistance.

4. Breathwork can clear the effects of birth trauma. Since the difficulties of birth are associated with the person's first breath, breathing is the most efficient way to access birth issues. A later chapter will be devoted entirely to early issues such as birth, prenatal life and conception.

5. Breathwork gives more access to positive feelings. For example, breathwork can dramatically improve the quality of one's sexual experience. It is an illusion to think that there is one faucet for our positive feelings and one for our negative feelings. All feeling comes out of the same faucet. Our only choice is whether we want to open the faucet, to grow more conscious. If the choice is made to open, we often get a rush of negative feeling first, followed by a clearer flow of positive feeling.

6. Ultimately, breathwork can connect the person to the boundless transpersonal dimension of life, to unity, and to a sense of kinship with oneself, others and the universe. Although I sit in meditation an hour a day, and have done so for nearly twenty years, I would say that at least half my most powerful spiritual experiences have come through breathing. Thousands of times in the two decades we have been using breathing, we have watched with awe and wonder as clients have journeyed into the transpersonal realm, feeling bliss, ecstasy, oneness and other lifechanging perceptions that are within us all.

Background

I discovered the power of breath quite by accident. One day, early in my career as a therapist, I worked with a woman who was experiencing some fears she sought to overcome. It was our first session, and after hearing her story, I noticed that she was expending most of her energy trying to control the fear, as if she had one foot on the accelerator and one on the brakes. Her body was stiff with tension, and her breathing was labored and controlled. I put my hand on her shoulder, and encouraged her to drop the resistance and let go into the actual experience of the feelings. With a whoosh her breathing released, becoming deeper and faster. She deeply contacted the fear, and began vibrating and shaking in the chair. I suggested she give free rein to her breath, letting it go as fast and deep as it wanted. Vibrations shook her whole body, continuing for several minutes. I had not witnessed anything like this before.

Having nothing to go on but my trust in her body's wisdom, I felt awed and scared. Something felt very right about what we were doing, though, and I encouraged her to stay with it as long as it felt comfortable to her. After a few minutes the shaking subsided, and she looked serene. In fact, she looked—radiant! It was hard to recognize her as the same tight-lipped, fright-eyed individual she had been twenty minutes earlier. When she could talk again, she said she felt confident and alive. In addition, she had thought of several creative solutions to the fears. I was moved; I had not seen such a rapid change in all the time I had worked with people.

I became thoroughly intoxicated with the power of the breath. During the following two years, I set for myself the goal of watching 100 people breathe, so I could learn about the process from the inside out. I participated in bioenergetics and Reichian therapy training, and read everything I could find from Eastern and Western psychology which had anything to do with breathing. In the mid-seventies I began using breathwork with individuals and groups, gradually evolving a set of instructions and procedures that allowed breathwork to take people through their personalities down into the boundless transpersonal space. In 1977 I began doing larger groups; now, over 100 participants are often breathing at the same time.

My focus throughout this time was to devise a process that truly fit contemporary lifestyles. I found techniques like rebirthing and Reichian therapy to be much too limited for what I felt could be accomplished through breathwork. Ultimately, I came to believe that the process hinges upon two essential conditions. The first absolute condition is the state of being of the therapist. How deep the client can go is determined by how far we as therapists are willing to go with ourselves. The second essential is to know a technique which can take people all the way—through personality, through emotion, through birth, to space. A focus on birth, as in rebirthing, or on sexual energy, as in Reichian therapy, are both important but focus too narrowly on specific phenomena. The ultimate payoff of correct breathwork is that it allows us to get beyond phenomena, to pure space.

The Therapist's State of Being

*W*ith the correct attitudes and intentions, our presence alone has healing value. If the therapist is fully present, there is virtually no limit to how much can be accomplished in a given session. The chief barrier to being present is that our own unresolved issues may emerge as the client breathes. As energy rises in the breather, so it does in the therapist. With experience, you will learn to recognize and handle your own material if it begins to emerge. Ideally, you will have done a great deal of your own breathwork, so that you will be able to stay present and clear as the client goes through all manner of phenomena. The next best thing is to become fluid at

15

handling blocks, both in yourself and in your client, so that you are nimble at getting unstuck when material emerges. For example, if your client is going through some fear and your own fear gets stirred up, as an experienced therapist you will know how to open up to his or her fear, breathe into it, love it and let it go. You can only learn how to do this through practice.

Throughout a breathwork session, the therapist must practice a loop of awareness that goes back and forth between therapist and client. You will not be able to do this flawlessly all the time. The mind's tendency is to be present, lose it, be present, lose it. During a session, you will likely get lost in your own thoughts, have unwelcome feelings emerge, get sleepy, and uncover any number of other phenomena. With experience, these things will occur less often, and you will be able to correct them quickly as they do.

The space created by therapists in themselves determines how much space clients can occupy. Space is defined as how much the therapist is willing to feel. Crucial to a therapist's development are the following questions:

- How open am I to my anger? Fear? Sadness?
- How comfortable am I with my sexuality?
- Am I trying to prove my adequacy?
- How open am I to the full range of energetic vibration in me?
- Am I willing for myself and others to be in direct contact with the universe?

In supervising therapists over the years, I have seen seemingly small adjustments in these issues have tremendous impact on how much money they make, how many clients they can see, and other indicators of effectiveness and success.

It is important to stay in touch with your own breathing during a session. Many times during the work I check in with my own breathing. Is it easy and full? Am I holding my breath, even subtly, on the in-breath or out-breath? Is my belly tight? If my breathing is restricted in any way, I open up to the reason, both in myself and my client.

In breathwork, it is important to keep awareness open and love flowing. There are places only love can go; wounds that only love can heal. Our job as therapists is to love the client's unlovable places, and our own. "Go beyond reason to love," is a thought that often comes to me as I work (gratitude to Thaddeus Golas for acquainting me with this notion). Understanding, which the mind prizes so highly, often comes only later.

If you are taking your client through a complete breathwork session, the following instructions are the most efficient I have found so far. Under no circumstances should you attempt to conduct breathwork sessions without training. For our schedule of training programs in how to do the work, write for our brochure.

Instructions For Individual Breathwork

1. Begin by having the person *lie down on his or her back.* Use a firm, but giving surface, such as a thick foam pad. The client may lie flat, or with knees up. It is best to remove jewelry, and to begin with a relatively empty stomach.

2. Review with the person the *intentions or goals* for the session. Discuss any *fears, questions or clarifications.*

3. Ask the person to *relax the jaw, open the throat and breathe in and out through the open mouth.* Use open-mouth breathing in the early stages, until the person masters an attitude of openness in the throat. Later the client can breathe through the nose, once the throat can stay open and relaxed. The throat is a key to the energy structure of the whole body. If the throat is relaxed and free, energy flows through the whole person. If the throat constricts, you will see constriction all the way down the body.

Individual Breathwork

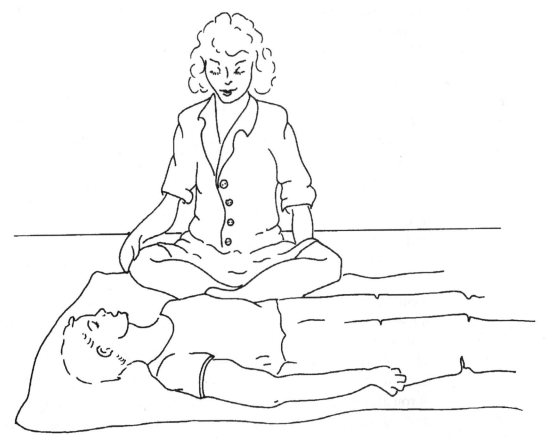

4. *Open the mouth wide enough to get one or two fingers between the upper and lower front teeth. Ask the client to relax the throat so that they can say a long AAA (on the in-breath)—HAAA (on the out-breath). Have them say it a few times out loud, then have them breathe in and out with a silent AAA-HAAA.* The sound of the air passing through the throat is a key diagnostic device. When the sound is open, deep, clear and full, it indicates that energy is flowing through the body in the optimal way. When it is shallow, ragged or hesitant, it means that the person is wrestling with a block.

   The body's energy structure can be compared to a garden hose with seven nozzles. The nozzles are around the eyes, jaws, throat, chest, diaphragm, belly and pelvis/buttocks. These places are sensitive areas of the body where tension lodges. As one proceeds down the body toward the pelvis, the nozzles regulate more and more energy. For this reason, it is best to open the blocks in a downward direction, making sure the throat is relaxed and open as the person breathes.

5. *Ask the person to breathe as fast or slowly as he or she wishes. Invite the client to establish a rhythm and be sensitive to its wanting to change pace.* If I sense that the person is breathing slowly in order to avoid feeling something, I will encourage him or her to speed up. Similarly, if I think the person is rushing because of a hurry-up program of some sort, I will ask him or her to slow down. Notice if the breathing has an effortful quality to it; if it does, invite the person to lighten it up, making it more relaxed and playful.

As the person breathes, add the following bits of information in small doses:

6. Suggest that the person *take each experience as it comes*, accepting whatever is there and flowing with whatever emerges. Most of the good things in breathwork come when the person lets go of control, even a little. At some point in a person's evolution, it is important to let go of judgment ("Is this the experience I'm supposed to be having?") and simply take things as they come. In breathwork we invite a person to adopt a body attitude of openness and willingness by relaxing the throat and breathing fully in and out.

7. Tell the person that *it is all right to lose awareness and the full, open breath.* There is no penalty for losing it; he or she should not attempt to hold onto the breath. Whenever the person notices losing it, simply pick it up again. It takes time to teach the energy system to handle more energy. Often, in fact, the person will only be able to take three or four full breaths before unconscious material begins to emerge.

   When the unconscious material begins to emerge, the open attitude in the throat will disappear, the breath will become shallow and constricted, and an emotion or a personality pattern will emerge. A pattern is any repetitive, programmed sequence of behavior such as getting sleepy, bored, feeling defensive, or getting scared. The energy of breathing has flushed the pattern to the surface. The material must be integrated at the body level before the person picks up the deep breathing again. By this we do not mean that the person must understand what has emerged, but simply that he or she has relaxed into it on the body level. The process of integrating may take only seconds.

The art in breathwork and life is not to avoid being stuck but rather to take things as they come, observing them closely and moving through them. Each act of opening invites the next block; each resolved block invites the next opening. With practice, ease develops until we are able to hold both openness and stuckness in a larger context of ourselves.

8. Tell the person that *both pleasant and unpleasant feelings turn into positive energy if experienced fully.* As we mentioned earlier, the full range of emotion—rage to bliss—comes out of the same faucet. Our only decision is whether or not to open the faucet. When we are fully open, all emotion turns to energy. Fear, anger and other feelings repeat themselves until we allow ourselves to experience them. Our task is to open ourselves to the full symphony of feeling—tympani to harp.

Oddly, humans have as much resistance to positive energy as they do to the negative. While practically everyone says that they prefer pleasure to pain, thousands of breathwork sessions have shown us that this is not true. I have seen people sob for an hour, but I have rarely seen anyone be able to sustain five minutes of ecstasy. Though we have had hundreds of experiences of handling negative energy, we are still kindergartners at learning to feel good.

9. *Tell people not to stop until they feel peace, bliss or an organic stopping place. Particularly, one should never stop in the midst of a block, or when one is feeling bad for any reason. Always breathe through it;* otherwise, the lesson will have to be repeated later. Peace and bliss are easy to recognize by the person's face. If they want to stop for any other reason, ask them if they are feeling any fear or discomfort in their body. If so, continue until it passes before stopping.

When completed:

10. *Make sure the person is grounded before leaving your presence.* Breathwork sometimes makes people feel spacy. Make sure the person can make eye contact and process information (such as stop signs) in the normal manner before leaving. Sometimes I send people out for a walk around the block before I let them drive. Light massage is grounding, as is drinking a glass of water or juice. Having the person send love to someone else, even if the other is a thousand miles away, is a sure way to get grounded. Love is the ultimate grounding tool, as it always puts the person back in balance.

Phenomena During Breathwork

*M*any different phenomena occur during breathwork; most are caused by the push of the building energy against the barriers in the body and the mind. Here are some of the most frequently occurring phenomena.

1. Probably the most common occurrence during breathwork is the *release of emotion*. A wave of sadness may come up, ranging in intensity from mild regret to deep sobs. A gust of anger may emerge, or a shudder of fear. Sexual feelings sweep the body, as do excitement and bliss. The useful attitude to take toward waves of emotion is to let them come, to be with them while they are there, and not to hold on to them as they subside. A deep experience of bliss may be just beyond a tidal wave of anger, and vice versa. We say: Take all emotions as they come, and don't try to hold on when they want to go.

2. *Losing the form.* When a block emerges during breathwork, the first thing that happens is that the person loses the full, deep breath. The throat and mouth close, or the breath becomes shallow and tentative. The deep breathing has flushed out a block, and the person has "gone unconscious" (i.e., unconscious material has emerged which has overshadowed the conscious intention to breathe deeply). The act of going unconscious is not wrong or to be resisted; it is the natural part of the process. Later, the person can glean the lesson to be derived from the event. For example, one may learn that the act of going unconscious always follows the emergence of a particular feeling, such as fear or sexual feelings. This insight may prove to be crucial in unraveling a troublesome life pattern.

3. *Going to sleep.* Occasionally a person will go completely to sleep, snores and all. This can mean that anesthesia is being released from the body, or that a very deep block is being accessed. At the end of a session, after a big release, it can simply signal deep relaxation.

4. *Tetany.* In breathwork a phenomenon called tetany happens on occasion. The symptoms: stiffness in the hands and feet, numbness, a tight band around the forehead, and the mouth drawing to an O. Tetany can occur when the rising energy hits a stubborn defense system, and it can occur when birth trauma is releasing. Sometimes it is simply due to the person taking a larger out-breath than in-breath.

   No matter what the cause, the therapist should tell the breather to relax into it, and feel the sensations, to go into it rather than contracting away from it in fear. Some common beliefs that underlie tetany are: I'm unwanted; nobody will take care of me; I don't deserve to be here; my presence causes trouble. The therapist can sometimes free a person from tetany instantly by saying things like "You're welcome here; you deserve to be here; you'll be taken care of."

5. Several other phenomena happen during breathwork. Some of these are flickering eyelids, coughing or choking, boredom, and a feeling of general stuckness. These are all signs of blocks releasing. In all these cases, the therapist must encourage the breather to breathe on through. A direct experience of energy is just on the other side of these events.

6. As blocks dissolve, energy is encountered. This is experienced as buzzing, tingling or humming, and an increased feeling of aliveness in the body. Reich called these waves of energy "streamings." They are highly desirable, as they signal the release of blocks in the bodymind. A stronger form of vibration, like a humming electric current, can sometimes be experienced. The strongest vibrations I have felt or witnessed are waves of intense shaking that pass up and down the body. Once I experienced this vibration so intensely that it flipped me around 90 degrees on the bed. The vibrations are typically experienced as deeply pleasurable and meaningful to the person.

7. When breathers can let go deeply enough, they may have a direct experience of space, a deep feeling of peace, clarity and resolution. Bliss often accompanies the sense of space. It is a feeling of ecstatic satisfaction that brings a smile to the whole body. The path to bliss and space is through opening up to all our feelings, positive or negative. Bliss and space are the pleasant surprises at the bottom of all feelings.

8. Deep breathwork often brings forth experiences that have a birth and/or conception flavor. In Radiance Breathwork, we do not program or push the breather to experience birth or conception, but rather we are open to it coming up organically. When it's time, the person will automatically begin releasing birth and conception material, but we do not recommend focusing on these areas as end goals. Other techniques such as rebirthing key in on birth as a primal event, which it certainly is, but there is little ultimate therapeutic value in simply re-experiencing birth. Approximately half our breathwork clients have had an earlier negative or incomplete experience with rebirthing or some other form of breathwork. It is important to know that all phenomena are just that—phenomena—and that the ultimate value of breathwork lies in its ability to take us beyond into space.

Therapeutic Interventions

*T*he primary tool is the state of being of the therapist. If you as therapist are humming with energy and love, you don't have to do much else. Other tools are handy to have around, though, for those times when you are not as keen as you could be.

Priming. During breathwork I often take an audible breath as a way of priming the pump. It reminds both the client and me to keep the breath deep and full. The sound of the breath is a more subtle reminder than a verbal phrase.

Touch. In our certification program we spend considerable time helping people learn when and how to touch. There are effective forms of deep and light touch, and places on the body where touch can trigger emotional release. Learning how to use touch requires hands-on instructions and fine-tuning, and is beyond the scope of the written word to explain. If you are drawn to learning to use breathwork as a professional, please correspond with us, and we will forward a schedule of upcoming training.

Verbal phrases. Verbal messages are useful in assisting people in getting through blocks, and for giving them support and encouragement in opening up to the full range of experience. A block may be understood in several ways. It may be an experience, such a feeling or a need, that has been sealed off. It is kept out of awareness by unconsciously tensing against it. A block may also be an out-flowing feeling such as love or compassion which has been thwarted through rejection or inhibition. It can also be a lesson or piece of wisdom that has been ignored. In any case, these issues find a place in the body, manifesting in tension or pain, and can be released through breathing. The verbal phrases we use are designed to align the conscious with the unconscious. Here are some phrases we often use:

"Let go into yourself."
"Can you love that?"
"Are you willing to experience that?"
"Keep coming back to a willing attitude."
"Love as much as you can from right where you are."

I once encountered a person holding up his hand during a large group breathing session, saying that he was feeling extremely nauseous. He did, indeed, look green. I asked him to let himself feel deeply just how sick he was rather than to resist it. Seconds later, the nausea completely disappeared and he was in bliss.

Love. Love is the most potent dissolver of blocks and the greatest healing power. It took me a long time to learn to let myself feel love. It was much longer before I could trust its healing power. One day I opened up to my most negative feelings and had the incredible experience of loving them. Those feelings dissolved and never came back. In that moment I saw that love is real and that I am the source of it, as are all of us.

In breathwork, I now rely on love above all else. I notice where a person is stuck—what isn't moving as they breathe—and focus love on that place. Sometimes I focus love with my mind, sometimes with touch. I see the most miraculous events unfold right after focusing love. For example, a person will be contorted in the agony of birth trauma, and I will remember to love them for being where they are. Seconds later the body uncurls, and a smile bathes the face.

Love is so powerful, yet I frequently forget it until I have exhausted everything else. Often I have tried everything I knew to get a person unstuck, with zero results. Then I will remember just to love them the way they are, stuck and all. The block soon dissolves, and the light breaks through. Of course, I forget the powerful simplicity of love until next time. But this is as it should be, for life and work at their best form a spiral of opportunities to learn and re-learn the transforming power of love.

Three Initial Breathing Activities

Often I do not begin with a cathartic Radiance Breathwork session. I use the following activities, depending on the needs of the client. I frequently work with people who are strangers to the power of breathing. They need to be introduced to it in gentle gradations. Sometimes clients have been breathing upside-down for so long that I have to get their breathing right side up before they can benefit from any deeper type of breathwork. By upside-down I mean that they keep their belly tight, forcing the breath up into the chest. Correct breathing is done with a relaxed belly, except in circumstances where actual fight or flight is called for, which is rare in modern life. In a correct breath the belly expands before the chest rises. Belly expansion indicates that the diaphragm is moving downward in the correct fashion. A lack of belly movement is a sure sign that the person is stuck in fight-or-flight breathing.

BASIC DIAPHRAGMATIC BREATHING

This first activity is designed to help the client establish free diaphragmatic breathing. When the breath comes in, the diaphragm should move downward, causing the abdomen to expand. When the breath goes out, the diaphragm moves upward, causing the belly to flatten. Many people have this pattern upside down. They tighten the belly on the in-breath, or even keep it tight regardless of their breathing, inflating the chest with each in-breath. This pattern is seen in a variety of complaints, such as asthma, depression, anxiety and other common issues people bring to therapists. It is one of the first things I look for in a initial session, because it can often be quickly treated with great benefit and relief for the client. What you will usually see is a breathing pattern where most of the breath is up in the chest, and where the belly does not expand appreciably with the in-breath. You want to establish a pattern where most of the breath is down in the belly, and where the chest does not move a great deal with the breath. Both should move, but the belly must be expanded before the breath turns up toward the chest.

Over two thirds of the blood circulation in the lungs is in the lower third of them. Over a quart of blood passes through here every minute, compared to less than a teacup at the top of the lungs. Full-scale asthmatics, for example, panic because they are not getting enough air (because they are not breathing down in their bellies), so they tighten their bellies even more and labor to take huge breaths up in their chests. The vicious circle continues until a drug is administered or they pass out. If they pass out, nature takes over and puts the breath back down where it is supposed to be. Many people have a miniature version of what the asthmatic feels as a life and death matter.

Here's the sequence of activities I use to help clients learn diaphragmatic breathing.

1. Invite the person to sit comfortably upright or lie down.

   Leaning back halfway, such as in a recliner, is not recommended because it tightens the abdominal muscles slightly. Make sure their hands are at their sides and their clothing is not restricting their breathing.

2. Ask them to put their hands just below the rib cage, as if they had their hands on their hips, only slightly higher. The fingers should be able to feel the muscles on either side of the navel. Have them tense and relax the belly muscles a number of times, until they can definitely feel the difference between a relaxed belly and a tight one. Invite them to feel the tightening with their fingers as well as their internal sensing. An image I use: "Imagine you are pulling a cork into your navel, back toward your spine. Then let it go." Have them gradually slow down the tensing and relaxing until it takes a few seconds to tighten and a few seconds to let go.

3. From here on out, ask them to keep their belly very relaxed. Notice when they are tightening, and remind them to relax. Say, "Breathe deeply and slowly in and out, feeling the rise and fall of your belly with your hands. Feel the belly expand on the in-breath, and empty on the out-breath. Let the belly fill fully before the breath turns

up into the chest." You may need to repeat this basic idea many times; after all, they may have been practicing wrongly 20,000 times a day most of their lives.

4. After a few minutes, have them relax their arms at their sides. Take a medium-weight book and place it over their navel. Ask them to keep the slow, deep belly breath going, and to feel the book rise and fall.

5. If they feel dizzy or in any way uncomfortable, have them back off to a gentler breath or pause entirely for a while until the uncomfortable sensation passes.

6. If they have learned it lying down, ask them to do it upright in a chair. It is a different sensation, which some people find harder. Start with the hands on the belly in the upright position, and progress to sensing it from inside without hands.

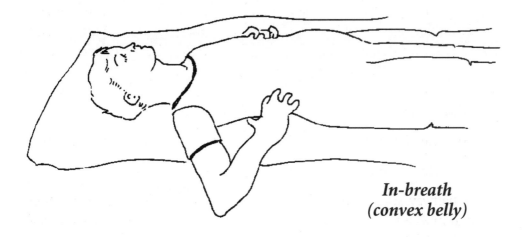

In-breath
(convex belly)

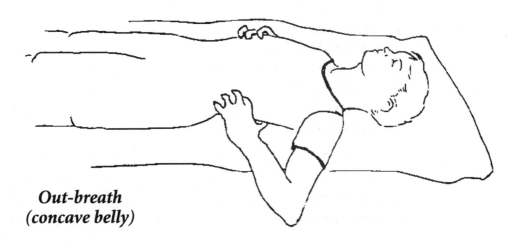

Out-breath
(concave belly)

RADIANCE BREATHING MEDITATION INSTRUCTIONS

The Radiance Breathing Meditation has several purposes. It is designed to expand your ability to experience positive energy. Every day you do the meditation, it will reset your body's energy thermostat at a higher level. Radiance Breathing Meditation will fill your body with waves of energy, and your mind with clear light. The smoother breathing rhythms you will develop in the Meditation can be used to breathe through stresses in daily life, such as feelings of anger, fear and sadness that often cause people to hold their breath. Ideally, you will practice the Meditation every day for 20-30 minutes. It is best done lying down, before you have eaten.

The Meditation brings up energy and light, and will clear out of your mind and body anything that is interfering with your ability to feel energy and light all the time. So, one person may bring up energy and light, then drop off to sleep instead of being able to consciously remain there. Another person may bring up energy and light, then feel tension in the neck. Still another may feel the urge to cry. In the Meditation you do not resist any of these experiences. If you drop off to sleep, enjoy it. If the neck gets tense, shift to the lighter breathing until it passes. If emotions well up, be with them until they pass and you are able to get back to the breathing again. With enough practice, you will develop the ability to stay suspended in the energy and light all the time.

Now, if you are ready to begin:

Lie down and get comfortable. Close your eyes and relax your whole body.

(Pause until the person is comfortable.)

Tense every muscle in your body. Feet, legs, buttocks, stomach, shoulders, fists, make a face, stretch your jaw, press your tongue to the roof of your mouth. Hold tightly . . . now let go completely and relax.

(5-second pause)

Now take three big breaths from your toes to your high chest, letting each go with an audible Haaaaaaa.

(Repeat the tense/relax sequence, including the three big breaths, three times.)

From now on, you'll be breathing in and out of your nose, and in and out of your relaxed abdomen. (If nose is stuffy, it's okay to breathe in and out of mouth; make sure throat is relaxed.) Breathe deeply and fully in and out of your abdomen . . . keep your muscles as relaxed as you can . . . breathe in fully, and let gravity breathe out . . . you can pull the in-breath, but avoid pushing the out-breath. (If the person can't get the abdomen to move, have them put their hands on the abdomen for feedback.)

(Let them take 10-12 breaths)

Now shift to a very quiet breathing, still in your abdomen. In the Radiance Breathing Meditation, you will go back and forth between a big breathing rhythm and a quiet, subtle rhythm. The big rhythm fills your body with energy and your mind with light, and the subtle rhythm lets your body integrate the energy. Notice if you feel sensations of Radiance: tingling, buzzing, humming, currents, breeze-like sensations. (Have them tell you out loud.) Notice the quality of light in your mind. Is it white light? Is it darkness? Is it a combination? Describe it for me out loud.

(After 30-60 seconds of quiet breathing)

Now go back to the big rhythm, and make it sound like this. (Model the in-out-rest, in-out-rest rhythm for them. About 60 beats per minute, or 1 cycle per 3 seconds. Have them pick up the rhythm and do it with them for 12 breaths). Now shift back to the subtle, quiet breathing. If you feel like taking a big breath in your chest now and then, that's fine. Generally, though, keep the breath in your abdomen.

(Ask again if they are experiencing Radiance sensations. Check on the quality of light in their mind. If there are no Radiance sensations or increase in light, on the next cycle have them breathe deeper and speed up the rhythm slightly. If the sensations are too strong, have them breathe slower and less deeply.)

Now return to the big rhythm (model again for them), and make it circular, keeping the in-breath connected to the out-breath with a gentle curve at the top of the in-breath. (Have them do 12 big breaths, then have them shift back to subtle. Ask about energy sensations. Also, notice if they are straining, pushing or holding the breath anywhere during the cycle. If so, give them feedback on this during the subtle breathing.)

Now go back to the big rhythm . . . relaxed, full, circular, connected . . . Go with the big rhythm until you feel it's time to shift to the subtle . . . Use your intuition, but be sure to go to the quiet breathing if the energy sensations become too strong, or if you feel anything unpleasant such as dizziness, tension or anything uncomfortable. If that happens, switch immediately to quiet breathing until it passes. Keep the breath primarily in your abdomen, although you may want to take a breath up in the chest now and then. As you breathe, keep the jaws and base of the tongue relaxed.

(Monitor them to make sure they don't charge into any big releases. Radiance Breathing Meditation is intended to teach them how to come up to energy and light, and stay suspended in it. With this practice, it's important to work the subtle edge, rather than bursting through. If something does slip through, such as emotional release or pain, have them go to the subtle, connected breathing in the abdomen until it passes.)

(While they are on quiet breaths, remind them to keep it connected and circular and smooth. If they drift off or space out, fine. When they come back, tell them it's fine to drift off, and have them take 10-12 big full-body breaths.)

(When you are ready to finish) When you come to a good stopping place, rest for a minute or two before opening your eyes. When you're ready to come back to your awareness of the room, take a few big breaths throughout your whole body, and release them with big Haaas. When you are practicing at home, use the big rhythm to bring up energy and light, then shift to the quiet rhythm to let the energy and light integrate. If emotions or tension or anything comes up, shift to the quiet breathing until these integrate. In the Radiance Breathing Meditation, you don't try to have catharses or blow-outs. Instead, allow the energy and light to integrate whatever comes up. This means you bring up energy and light, then shift to the quiet breathing to allow it to integrate. Then, you go back to the big rhythm again. Do this as many times as you like, using your intuition to tell you when it's time to shift.

Remember as you are going around in your daily life to take connected, rhythmic breaths in your abdomen. Whenever you are under stress, or when you want to feel better, go to the deep, full, connected, rhythmic breathing in your abdomen.

(Walk around for grounding; talk with them about their experience. Go over the basics so they can practice at home.)

INSTRUCTIONS FOR THE INTERMEDIATE PRACTICE

Two criteria must be met before teaching the intermediate practice. First, the person must have had clear experiences of staying suspended in energy and light with no negative phenomena (tension, pain, dizziness, unpleasant emotions) emerging. This indicates that the person can handle energy successfully, and is on the way toward healing his or her emotional issues. If he or she still has negative phenomena emerging, have the person continue the basic practice until he or she can bring up energy without negativity of any kind.

The second criterion is that the person's breathing rhythm be smooth and connected. This may be observed by watching the abdomen rise and fall with the breath. If it is ragged, hesitant or labored, he or she must continue with the basic practice until it has been smooth and connected for a while.

If they are ready for the intermediate practice, have them begin with the previous instructions, and add the following instructions about ten minutes into the practice. Always add new instructions during a period of quiet breathing.

Put a smile on your face . . . one that feels very pleasant to you. If you like, you can think of something pleasant. Make it an authentic smile . . . get the feeling of the smile in your face. (When the smile is in place, continue.)

Now keep the smile on your face, and transfer it to your eyes . . . transfer the smile to your throat, too . . . (pause) . . . bring the smile to your chest and heart . . . bring the smile to your abdomen . . . up your back. Smile in all these places as you breathe. Go to the big rhythm now, and smile into the energy.

(Pause. When they have shifted back to the quiet breath, add the following:)

Check your smile . . . face . . . eyes . . . throat . . . chest . . . abdomen . . . pelvis and buttocks . . . back . . . get the smile in all those places . . . and if any other area comes to your attention, smile into that place also . . .

(After five minutes or so, add the following:)

Now relax your jaw, open your mouth and relax your throat. For a while now, breathe through your open mouth. Let the breath come in and out with an Aaa-Haa sound. Take twelve breaths this way and then shift to the quiet breathing through your nose.

(Pause)

Keep bringing the smile to your body and mind. Now go back to the big rhythm through the open mouth. Go back and forth between the big rhythm and the subtle rhythm as your intuition directs you. Bring up light and energy with the big rhythm, then shift to the subtle rhythm until it integrates.

(Have them continue as long as they wish, or time allows, then have them take a few big breaths from toes to high chest, saying Haaaa on the exhale, then come back.)

INSTRUCTIONS FOR THE ADVANCED PRACTICE

The criterion for moving to the Advanced Practice is that the person has smooth breathing with no effort, along with consistently positive experiences. If negative phenomena that feel unpleasant to the person are still emerging, keep practicing the basic and intermediate forms until these phenomena are smoothed out.

Add the following instructions before the person begins breathing.

The Advanced Practice brings a stronger experience of energy to the body, and we need to spend more time releasing tension, so the flow of energy won't be impeded. Tense every muscle in your body . . . feet . . . legs . . . pelvis . . . buttocks . . . hunch your shoulders . . . make fists . . . make faces . . . alternately squint your eyes and open them wide . . . press your tongue to the roof of your mouth . . . hold . . . now release with a big sigh and Haaaaa.

(Pause ten seconds.)

Now repeat this twice more on your own.

(When ready to continue:)

Now we will be releasing more tension from specific armor segments . . . Alternately open wide and clench shut your eyes . . . while you're doing this, alternately clench your jaw and open wide . . . Make every movement different . . . move your jaw from side to side also . . . look from side to side and all around with your eyes . . . thrust your jaw forward and back . . . continue for a minute or two . . . go on through the point of tiredness.

(Pause)

Now alternate between low hums and the highest sounds you can make. Let your tongue move loosely around, making nonsense sounds like la-la-la. Combine this with stretching and clenching the jaw, and moving it side to side and jutting it forward. Take it to the limit, no holding back.

(Let this continue for 1-2 minutes.)

Now pull air into your chest, hold it and pull your shoulders up high while pulling your chest and stomach up and in. Hold in for ten seconds and let go with a big sigh. Now shake your hands rapidly, letting your wrists be very loose. Pause for a few breaths before repeating.

(Continue for one to two minutes.)

Now alternate turning your head, as if saying No, from side to side as far as it will go . . . then nod Yes in an exaggerated up and down movement . . . make the movements slowly . . . go back and forth between the Yes and the No.

(Continue for one to two minutes.)

Lift your legs off the ground five or six inches, then swing them to the outside . . . Hold them there, and rotate the feet slowly. Hold until tired, then let them relax. Take a few breaths and repeat.

(Continue for one to two minutes.)

The breathing will be done through the relaxed jaw and open mouth. Breathe into the abdomen through your mouth . . . Bring the breath in and let it go in a circular, full, relaxed way . . . Connect the in-breath to the out-breath . . . Use the in-out-rest rhythm, one cycle every three seconds . . . Do this four times, then go to the subtle breath through the nose. Let it sound like you're saying a big AA-Haaaa.

(Pause and ask about Radiance sensations.)

Now take eight open-mouth breaths, then shift to the subtle breathing through the nose. On the last big breath, let it come up high into your chest. Let your pelvis rock with the breath, and smile into the sensations of Radiance.

(Pause; ask about energy sensations. If they're too strong, shift back to four big breaths. If they're okay, keep repeating eight big breaths for a while, then give them permission to go back and forth according to their intuition. Remind them to shift to the subtle if anything uncomfortable emerges. After about ten minutes of practice, when the person is feeling clear, strong Radiance sensations, add the following:)

Now when you go to the subtle breathing, add sound to it. Breathe in through the nose, and go Hmmmmm on the out-breath. Let the Hmmmm on the out-breath be as long as the breath lasts. Find the tone or note that feels most pleasing to you. Let the Hmmmm resonate all of you, going especially to any areas that need healing. Smile with the Hmmmmm.

(After about five minutes, add:)

Now shift the mantra into your mind only. Let it find its own subtle rhythm. Feel free to let it come and go effortlessly. Don't try to hold onto it . . . when you notice it's gone, effortlessly come back to it. Continue to breathe in a subtle, connected way.

(After ten minutes or so, end with:)

Now just rest for two or three minutes, and let your attention turn back to the outside again. After two or three minutes, open your eyes and sit up. Remember, as you go around in life, to come back now and then to the connected, rhythmic breathing in your abdomen. When you're under stress, or when you want to feel better, go to the connected, rhythmic breathing in your abdomen.

Breathwork Protocol for Treating Clients in Physical Pain

A certain number of clients come in with physical pain. The pain can take many forms: headache, backache, sports-related soreness, or the fallout from an accident. A combination of touch and breathwork we have developed is very effective in reducing physical pain in clients. It gives a great deal of diagnostic information, and usually results in a state of deep relaxation and bliss in clients. Before using this protocol, make sure that there are no medical interventions that need to be made. If you or the client are in any doubt whatsoever, a medical referral should be made.

To illustrate, here is a clinical example of how the procedure works. A 40-year-old woman had an automobile accident in which another car crashed into the side of hers. No bones were broken, but she had a great deal of pain up and down her body. The focus of the pain was her neck, but her shoulders, arms and buttocks also hurt. She had approximately ten sessions of chiropractic, which gave her some relief, but she said the core of the problem was still in her body. She had gone to an orthopedist, who prescribed pain medication, but she resisted taking it because she did not like the depressant effects in the rest of her life.

Using the present protocol, she was given five sessions of treatment, after which she was pain-free. Here's how it was accomplished. In the first session, we made a body map of where the pain resided. This was done by having her first lie down on a massage table on her back. We carefully touched her with our fingers, beginning with the head and neck, and working down. We asked her to signal by saying "Yes" whenever she felt pain to our touch. We noted on the map where the hot spots were, the places where she said the most pain resided. This procedure took about twenty minutes, as, to her surprise, she had places of pain of which she was not aware all the way down to her heels and feet.

Then, in the half hour remaining in the session, we asked her to develop deep, relaxed breathing; we asked her specifically to breathe into her pain as we touched her. We asked her to tell us to stop if she felt she was contracting from the pain. Then we began systematically touching each spot to the level at which she could breathe into it. Several times we went too deep and she contracted, but in general we were able to stay at the appropriate level while touching each of the forty or so spots we had noted on the map. Throughout the procedure we reminded her to keep the breathing full, relaxed and deep, and to go out to meet the pain with her breath. We made three rounds of her body, beginning at the top of the front, working down the front to the feet, then up the back to the neck and head. So, by the end of the session, she had experienced something quite unique: 120 experiences of having her pain touched with care, and breathing into and through the pain. At the end of the fifty minutes, she looked and felt very different. There was color in her face, life back in her eyes, and as she put it, "light at the end of the tunnel." Although there was still pain in her body, she said she felt 100 percent better.

In the subsequent four sessions, we carried out the same procedure, and the results were that the pain gradually faded from her experience. Along the way, she sobbed during several sessions, got angry once, and fell deeply asleep several times. She was scheduled for a sixth appointment, but decided to cancel it because she felt the problem was solved.

The steps in the protocol are:

1. Make a body map of the pain spots. Actually mark these on a page-size tracing of the human body (or a photocopy of page 34). Indicate the intensity of the pain, which can be done by using different colors or numbers. Ask the person to say "Yes" each time you touch a spot that hurts. Doing this serves two functions. First, it indicates what hurts. Second, it gives the person a number of experiences of saying "Yes" to pain, beginning the flow of positive energy back into the hurt places.

2. Sitting at the person's head, place your fingers on the frontal eminences of his or her forehead. Invite the person to breathe in and out in a deep, relaxed rhythm. Stay in this position for one minute, while continuing to have them breathe in a gentle, connected rhythm. After one minute, you can take your fingers off the frontal eminences.

3. Begin touching each of the pain spots to the level at which they are aware of the pain. Invite the client to tell you if you are touching too hard. You want to make the person aware of the pain, but not to push so hard that he or she contracts. Touch each spot to the level at which the pain is felt but does not disrupt the breathing.

4. Work down the front and up the back. Make several rounds of the body, touching only for five to ten seconds per spot.

5. If fallout occurs (e.g., sobbing, reliving a memory), stay with it until it subsides, rather than pressing on.

6. At the end of the session, let the client rest for about two minutes, then end.

33

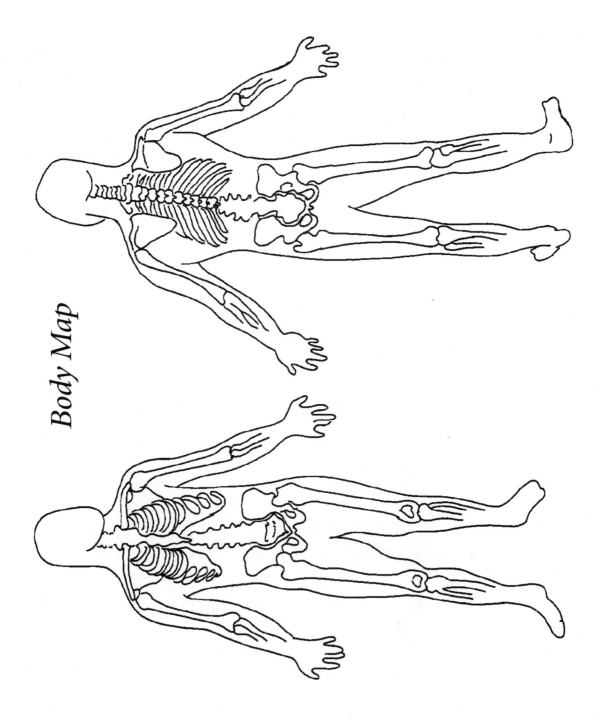

Body Map

34

Conclusion

Over the past twenty years of working with people I have come to have a deep, loving regard for the power of breath. I can understand why ancient students of consciousness like the Greeks used the same word for soul and breath. On the other side of the world, haole (pronounced howl-ee) is the Hawaiian word for the islanders' white visitors. One of the meanings of this word is "people without breath." Apparently the natives were quick to notice that their new guests did not breathe very well. Breathing was so important to the islanders that their word for family, ohana, translates in part as "people who breathe together."

I invite you to rediscover the power and glory of breathing, and join the large ohana of breathers across the world.

CHAPTER THREE

Leading Radiance Group Breathwork

Group breathwork is very powerful, because the energy generated by all the participants has a synergistic effect. In individual breathwork, it is up to the breather and the therapist to generate the energy that will allow the changes to take place. In a group, each breather may draw upon the cauldron of energy created by all participants. This effect allows for powerful and rapid transformations to take place. We have done breathwork in groups ranging from six people to over one hundred, and as the numbers increased, so did the energy. Breathwork in groups is so powerful that we have devised a separate set of instructions to make it a safe and integrative experience for all concerned. It is very easy to bring about a strong altered state of consciousness through group breathwork. However, it requires much more refined intentions to make it a valuable and effective experience.

Breathwork has become popular in recent years, and inevitably a number of ill-trained people have begun to practice it. Many people have asked us how to evaluate the experience of group leaders. In breathwork, perhaps the most important criterion is that leaders should have done a great deal of work with their own breathing. We have done four to five hundred personal sessions, and we recommend that leaders complete many such sessions with their own breathwork before leading groups. Experience with yoga, psychedelics and other techniques are not suitable substitutes. Our recommendation is to make sure to ask group leaders how many sessions they have done themselves. In our certification program, for example, our graduates have as much experience in their own work as they do in facilitating others. Without substantial personal experience with breath, facilitators are not able to create the proper ambience for the deepest work to take place.

For a valuable and integrative experience, attention first needs to be given to set and setting.

Set

e begin a group breathwork session with a discussion of the major phenomena that are likely to be encountered. Some of these are mentioned in the previous chapter on individual breathwork. Be sure, however, to discuss them in a group setting before the breathing begins. Knowing about these elements of breathwork helps create a safe context for these events to be experienced and breathed through.

1. *Emotional release.* Sadness, fear, anger, joy and sexual feelings are some of the emotions that come up during breathwork. When they arise, simply feel them deeply and don't try to hold on to them. It is best not to stop to analyze feelings encountered during breathwork. Analysis can best be done later, even over the next couple of days.

2. *Tingling, buzzing, humming, currents and vibration in the body.* These are all signs of energy moving in the body. When they happen, relax into them, avoid resisting them, and enjoy the experience. When tension begins releasing from the body, strong vibrations may shake the legs and other parts of the body. The vibration may range from fine shivers to bone-rattling shaking. These signs are always positive and should be relaxed into.

3. *Tetany.* When the mounting energy runs up against the body's habitual holding patterns of contraction, tetany often happens. The hands become numb and stiff, the extremities feel pins and needles, the mouth draws to an O, and a tight band emerges across the forehead. Sometimes this phenomenon is due simply to the person taking a longer out-breath than in-breath, and sometimes it is due to the emergence of birth trauma. When it occurs, the breather must relax into it and not try to resist it. If the breather continues to relax into it, the tetany will release. If tetany is resisted and fought, it can stay literally for hours.

4. *Bliss and unity.* Many people experience bliss and unity through breathwork. These feelings often come over the breather just after successfully releasing a block or feeling an emotion. Bliss and unity are among the premium payoffs for doing breathwork.

5. *Other phenomena.* People often have birth and conception experiences in breathwork. Again, it is best to participate with these events as they arise, not to stop and think about them. Resisting the power of a birthing experience that is trying to unfold within you is fruitless. Surrender and let it take you and your ego-mind on a ride. On

occasion people have more exotic phenomena, such as telepathic experiences and recollections that seem to come from a past life. These latter experiences could be fantasy, or they could come from accessing genetic memory banks. No one knows at present, but we encourage people not to get caught in any particular belief system. Those who promote the concept of reincarnation as if it were a certainty do a disservice to participants by encouraging them to lock into a particular belief system. Breathwork, at its best, takes people beyond belief systems to a direct encounter with energy. Indulgence in belief systems slows down the individual's evolution.

6. *Realizations.* Most people have awarenesses that come up either during breathwork or later. These realizations are sometimes purely physical, as in "I realized how tense my shoulders have always been." Other times they are emotional ("I felt deep sadness about my father's death, which I've never let myself feel") and spiritual ("I experienced complete oneness with everything, followed by waves of bliss"). Often the most profound awarenesses come a few days later. When one is working at the deeper levels, language cannot keep up with experience. It is only after a few days that the mind can assemble the experience into a meaningful structure.

Setting

The first group breathwork sessions took place in the cramped quarters of a therapy office. Since then, we have done them in hotel ballrooms, high school gyms, Esalen group rooms, churches and hospitals. The physical setting is not as important as the space created by the facilitators; what is important is that the participants feel safe and comfortable. We recommend that breathers wear comfortable clothing and eat only lightly before breathwork. We ask participants to bring mats, blankets and pillows, along with anything else they need to feel at ease.

There was an era when people brought flowers to sessions, followed by a crystal phase. Now people are bringing assorted talismans. Anything goes, so long as it doesn't interfere with breathing. One woman was attempting to breathe with a cross on her chest about the size and weight of a horseshoe. After discussing the metaphorical significance of this burden, she removed it and had a breakthrough session.

Music

Music plays an important role in our group sessions. A group breathwork session follows a pattern which begins with focus and concentration and is followed by mounting intensity, a climax, and finally a resolution or coming-down phase.

At the end, we ask the participants to move around, walk and talk in order to become grounded. The music that is chosen should reflect these phases. Here is a selection of music that we have found useful.

Focus and concentration phase (approximately the first 20-30 minutes of the session):
- Erik Satie, *Trois Gymnopedies*
- George Winston
- Ray Lynch, *Deep Breakfast* and *The Sky of Mind*
- Georgia Kelly, *Seapeace*
- Chris Spheeris, *Desires of the Heart*
- Robert Clark, *Improvisations*

Emotional release and drama phase:
- Vangelis, *Mask*
- Alan Hohvaness, *Mysterious Mountain*
- Vaughan Williams, *Theme from Thomas Tallis*
- Holst, *The Planets*
- Kitaro, *Tunhuang* and *Ki*
- Tangerine Dream, soundtrack from *Thief*
- Klaus Schulze, *X*, especially *Ludwig II*
- Constance Demby, *Novus Magnificat*

Coming-down phase:
- Samuel Barber, *Adagio for Strings*
- Pachelbel's *Canon in D*
- Vangelis, *Apocalypse Des Animaux* and *Ignacio*
- Cutler and Jones, *Kali's Dream* and *Awake and Dreaming*

Grounding and movement phase:
- Michael Schrieve and Klaus Schulze, *Transfer Station Blue*
- Jean Michel Jarre, *Oxygene* and *Equinoxe*
- Andreas Vollenweider
- Greek dance music
- African drumming, e.g., Olatunji

Facilitators

*W*e use two types of facilitation in group breathwork sessions. The first type is facilitation by peers. We ask participants to find a partner and decide who wants to breathe first. The breather lies down, with the sitter at his or her side. The job of the sitter is to hold the breather in a space of love, acceptance and healing. The intentions of the sitter are important. With correct intentions, the breather has an unlimited amount of space for healing, while narrow intentions can thwart the power of the experience. There is one key intention that makes the difference. The sitter must have the core intention that the breather can go through any experience to completion. Inexperienced sitters get scared halfway through a deep process on the part of the breather and are often tempted to jump in, fix the person, and make them feel better. Often, though, the breather must go through deep pain and stuckness before coming out into the light. If the sitter rushes in and tries to make the person feel better right in the midst of a deep release, it can make the breather slam on the brakes. Any intervention that is useful must come from a "You can go all the way" attitude. We emphasize this point to sitters at the beginning of a session.

A second type of facilitation comes from the leader(s) of the group. We have found that a ratio of twelve breathers to one leader is about the maximum for allowing the leader to keep track of all that is going on. In the early years of my career I would sometimes lead groups of 20-50 with no assistants. I usually decided about halfway through the session that I would never do it again and that I was in the wrong line of work. Still, it took me a dozen or so experiences of that nature before I always remembered to make sure I was well assisted.

Some of the activities of facilitators are practical; others are spiritual. People may need help or have questions during the breathing, and facilitators can circulate to take care of these needs, such as water or tissues. Sometimes facilitators can help people through deep spaces by providing love and support, both verbally and telepathically, as they are going through changes. Also, we have specific technical procedures facilitators use to help people through birth trauma.

In our certification program, we teach a form of bodywork that can be very useful to hasten people through stuck places. The facilitator, by touching certain places on the body, can often bring about a release that otherwise might be unattainable.

Outline for a Group Breathwork Session

1. Begin with a circle of hands. After you separate contact, have participants and leaders introduce themselves. A useful framework is to have people say their names, how they are feeling, and what they want from the session.

2. Leaders outline the purpose of breathwork and the types of experiences people have. This information is contained in the chapter on individual breathwork as well as in this chapter.

3. Questions and answers, discussion, sharing.

4. Break into pairs, each pair deciding who will breathe and who will sit.

5. Start music, and go through basic breathing instructions (from Chapter Two).

6. Remind sitters to create an atmosphere of allowing completion and non-interference for the breather. Remind them to do their best to stay open and loving toward themselves and the breathers.

7. Follow the energy in the room with appropriate music.

8. Remind breathers to raise their hands if they need help.

9. As partners complete the session, have them walk around, make contact, share experiences.

10. After people have finished, form a circle and have an opportunity for participants to talk about anything they wish to the whole group.

11. End with a circle of hands.

CHAPTER FOUR

Techniques for Clearing Birth, Prenatal and Conception Issues

A growing body of evidence, both experimental and clinical, has shown that many psychological problems can be traced back to events before and during birth. If we as therapists understand the impact of conception, prenatal and perinatal times, we are in a much stronger position to help our clients. The work we are evolving at our institute is designed to work directly with birth and earlier events to clear away the negative effects of trauma from these crucial imprints in our development.

In deep therapy experiences over the years, clients have reported phenomena that seemed clearly related to birth and even earlier experiences. At first we met this with disbelief, only later discovering the thirty or so years of scientific evidence demonstrating the impact of pre- and perinatal events on personality development. In fact, it was extraordinarily exciting (and something of a relief) to find confirmation in the scientific literature for our clinical findings, which seemed so radical that we were somewhat nervous about sharing them.

To begin, we will describe several examples which illustrate how we came to embrace a birth/prenatal/conception paradigm.

A woman, 27 years old, sought therapy because she had suddenly begun having anxiety attacks in airport concourses and shopping malls. In taking her history we found that the attacks began shortly after the birth of her first child the previous year. This woman had been heavily anesthetized during childbirth, as had her mother while giving birth to her. In addition, her neck and shoulders were quite tense, and her head cocked to the side as she spoke. These elements alerted us to the possibility that the birth of her son had somehow triggered a replay of her own birth trauma 27 years before. First, the anxiety occurred most strongly in environments that bore a metaphorical resemblance to the birth canal (shopping malls and airport concourses). Second, the anxiety was triggered by a birth event. Third, her body posture indicated a characteristic birth trauma pattern (head cocked to one side, tension in neck and shoulders) that we have found in hundreds of individuals over the years.

To solve the problem, we first used a number of birth metaphors in conversation with her. Among these were "It sounds as if you feel stuck," and "It must feel really good to get out into the light after being in a mall." At these, she perked up, indicating that we really understood what she was saying. In fact, she said that none of the healing professionals she had consulted seemed to understand what she was really saying. The use of birth metaphors with a client suffering the effects of birth trauma often provides instant bonding and trust. The treatment consisted of several elements. We taught her relaxation techniques that she could use at home or anytime she felt anxious. In the next session, we worked to release the neck and shoulder tension, using breathing and direct touch on the tense places. This procedure took several more sessions, with more intense feelings of the anxiety coming out each time. Then, a session of marital counseling was needed to handle issues that the anxiety, and its release, triggered in her husband. By this time her anxiety had abated, and there was much greater flexibility in her neck and shoulders. At this point she terminated, and flew to Scandinavia for a vacation.

A second case illustrates a typical occurrence in prenatal work: A troublesome feeling, which has resisted treatment, is healed through working at the prenatal level. A 61-year-old psychiatrist had a feeling of embarrassment or shame that had not yielded to other forms of exploration such as psychotherapy or bodywork. In a session of the prenatal therapy (to be described later in the chapter) it was determined that this feeling was actually something that his mother had experienced while he was in utero. After one session the feeling disappeared and has not to date returned.

A third example illustrates the relationship between a perinatal event and a current life issue which would seem on the surface to have nothing at all to do with birth. A woman, 40, came to therapy initially to resolve sexual issues she had with her husband. She had developed feelings of distance and numbness at the time her teenage daughter wanted to leave her mother and stepfather to live with her natural father. We worked with this client on connecting the feelings of numbness with unfinished feelings about her ex-husband. He had dropped her off at the hospital to give birth to her daughter and had told her at that time he was leaving the marriage and never wanted to see her again. It took three sessions of breathwork and movement to get down through several layers of old anger and hurt. In her fourth session she began to feel very cold, and her breath became labored and gargling. We encouraged her to breathe into the sensation, and she went into deep sobs. She connected the sadness and the coldness with the feelings she had felt at her daughter's birth. She continued to cry and breathe deeply, as vibration spread throughout her body. At this point, feeling her mother's ambivalence about having her, she realized that the sensation of coldness originated at her own birth. She said that smoking, which she was trying to quit, was related to a choking sensation in her throat.

After she had completed the cycle, she remembered two other incidents from the past year, both connected to her daughter's visits with the father. Each time she had felt a peculiar feeling in her head, and on one occasion she had fainted. All the events seemed linked to the birth matrix.

The following example illustrates how a person can cycle through birth, prenatal and conception events in a single session. In breathwork with a 38-year-old woman, a memory arose from when she was two years old: a man standing over her, violating her. As the breathwork deepened, she went back further to her own birth. She said she felt that she was a problem, innately wrong. Her birth had been difficult, and in fact she had always felt sluggish and angry. Her current problems had begun when her own daughter was born, after which she had felt depressed for two years. As she opened up to the deep feelings she was experiencing as she breathed, wriggling movements spontaneously began throughout her body. In our work we identify those movements as conception events, a distant reflection of the sperm's journey toward the egg. We invited her to participate with those movements as she breathed. As she did, it flashed into her mind that her feelings of unwantedness and wrongness had been part of her since the original union of sperm and egg. She screamed "I'm a mistake. A total, utter mistake." Sobs engulfed her and she curled up with her ancient sadness streaming through her body.

Then, we invited her to go inside a long fabric tube we keep on hand for such occasions. It is an excellent way of stimulating birth memories. At first she "couldn't stand" the fabric against her skin. Then she began a sequence of feelings that included being very energetic, then very sleepy, then defiant. She was emphatic that she wanted to do it her way, and she did, wriggling finally out into the light with a weary grin on her face. After a few more minutes of crying, she returned to her breathing and ended the session on a peaceful note.

Later, she recounted a recurring dream that she had dreamed since childhood.

> I am standing on the near side of a small lake or park. I am looking across the pond, longingly, to my family on the other side. They are having a picnic and seem happy and complete without me. They are oblivious to my presence. I long to get to the other side to be with them, but I am stranded on the near side. In order to be with them I have to get around the pond. In the lake are large fishes and monsters, and around the side the ledge is nar-

row. One monster is particularly threatening to me. It glides through the water with its neck sticking up above the water. This neck, or throat, is a long, narrow, transparent tube and this throat reveals everything the monster takes into his mouth and is swallowing. I can see bits of blood, tissue, flesh and guts going down the tube. I am terrified of this monster. He will eat me, too, if I venture out around the pond. I call out to my family for help, but they seem oblivious of me. They go about their picnic. I am helpless and alone and very scared.

We asked her to move with the dream, becoming the various parts. When she began to move with the monster she became nauseous and started gagging. Encouraged to continue gagging, she experienced a surge of feelings and had difficulty breathing. Mucus and tears poured from her eyes and nose. It then became clear to her that the dream was related to her own birth. It was a metaphor for how she felt in her family, and it was also related to her passage down the birth canal.

Diagnostic Indications That Birth, Prenatal and/or Conception Events Are Emerging

Clients with prenatal issues look and sound quite different from those with perinatal issues. Conception presents a third picture. Of course, many clients have all three types of issues, so the diagnostic signs are often intermingled.

Clients who are replaying elements of their birth often use birth metaphors in their speech. The word "pressure" comes up frequently in their conversations, as well as "jammed," "stuck," and "can't get out." They often feel rattled by change. Certain physical symptoms are common among clients who are reliving birth. They tend to have histories of respiratory distress, such as asthma, strep throat, bronchitis, allergies and chronic colds. Breathwork will often elicit congestion and a copious discharge of mucus. Stress often triggers headaches, dizziness and head pressure. Clients who were heavily anesthetized at birth may tend to get sleepy in stressful situations. Sometimes during breathwork they will go sound asleep just as energy is releasing in their bodies. A head torque to one side will often be found in those who had forceps deliveries.

The client with prenatal issues has an entirely different feel. Much of their language has an "as if" quality. They seem one step removed from themselves and the environment. They often report mood swings and feelings that arise seemingly from nowhere. Often, closer examination will reveal that these feelings actually belonged to their mothers, and they experienced them secondhand in utero. The client with prenatal issues often has a whole-body feeling of unwantedness or unlovedness, and frequently complains of not belonging and of having difficulty getting close to people. For example, one woman said, "I have a blank space when I think of love; I just don't know what it is." They often report, as one client did, that they feel an "innate sense of wrongness, as if whatever (they) do is never going to be good enough."

Conception is harder to distinguish in the client's presenting conversation or symptoms. The conception material often does not emerge until the client has accessed birth in the session. Often at the end of a birth sequence, which can take a few seconds or an hour, conception movements will emerge spontaneously. These may be the wriggling, swimming motions of the sperm, or the outreaching arms and circular movements of the egg. We most often diagnose the presence of conception through movements rather than observations of the breathing pattern.

Treatment Issues and Procedures

*W*e have evolved several procedures for directly working on conception, pre- and perinatal problems in clients.

USING BIRTH AND PRENATAL METAPHORS IN VERBAL THERAPY

In the initial stages of therapy, when trust is being established, we have found it very useful to use birth and prenatal metaphors in talking to clients. If the issues with which the clients are dealing are birth and/or prenatal in origin, they will often respond positively when relevant metaphors are used. Such metaphors are:

> "Sounds like you're feeling really stuck."
> "This issue really has you jammed up."
> "Is there any light at the end of the tunnel?"
> "It'll feel really good when you pull yourself out of this."
> (Prenatal) "It must feel as if you're all awash in this."
> "You must feel as if you're at the mercy of everyone else."
> (Conception) "It must feel as if you've been unhappy from the first moment

of your life."

> "It sounds like you operate out of a basic decision that you don't deserve to

be here at all."

These are only examples; it is up to the creativity of the therapist to deliver the relevant metaphor which fits the client's situation. While there are broad similarities, each person has a unique birth, prenatal and conception signature.

DIRECT BODYWORK

We use a number of bodywork strategies to bring up and resolve issues related to birth. We use deep stimulation on two zones, the jaws and heels/feet, to bring up perinatal issues. A more gentle form of pressure is used on the head. By placing the hands on the head and providing compression in a specific way, birth issues may be readily brought into the client's awareness. We also use acupressure, trigger point therapy and massage.

RADIANCE BREATHWORK

For clearing birth issues, we have found nothing more powerful than the type of breathwork we have developed and used since the mid-seventies. This process is described in two earlier chapters. Breathwork is not as effective for eliciting prenatal and conception events, because breath was not a factor in those moments of life. Movement was always present, however, and so we have devised a special form of movement work which we call—

RADIANCE MOVEMENT THERAPY

Radiance Movement Therapy is a process by which clients enter into a direct, moving dialogue with their inner selves. It accesses the body's innate intelligence and allows long-held patterns of movement to unfold into new patterns. A person with birth, conception or prenatal trauma has difficulty with change itself. Since life is based entirely on movement, a difficulty with change can be life-threatening. Movement work can help bring the client home to a more comfortable relationship with gravity and with the emotions held and expressed by the musculature. A person's style of movement will express whether he or she was held back, pulled by forceps or heavily anesthetized. It is remarkable and touching to see a person begin with a simple movement, such as moving the head in the direction of its characteristic twist, and then go deeply into reliving birth trauma within a few minutes.

We often begin the movement work with a dream. Since both dreams and movement are bridges between the conscious and unconscious, they make a powerful team. Here is a sequence of work with a woman, age 27, who was about to get married. The dream she brought in was violent: She had grabbed a boy's penis, and he had retaliated by kicking her sharply, which left a horrible pain in her belly.

We asked her to move as the little boy, becoming his qualities. She immediately felt two aspects of him: one brilliant and knowing, and the other, sneaky and powerful. When asked, she said the sneaky part of herself was anger, and the brilliant part was her will. We asked her to paint her will around her in space. She outlined a shape with her hands, describing it as a bubble. She said the bubble had always been there, six to twelve inches out from her body, and that it is always filled with the smoke of one to three cigarettes. When asked if the smoke barrier was permeable, she heard this question as pressure from the therapist to get rid of it. Tears poured out. She would not feel safe without it; it had always been there. At the end of the session the client said she had never smoked, but her mother had smoked heavily when pregnant with her.

RADIANCE PRENATAL PROCESS

We found that some clients could not resolve certain issues on land. So we evolved the Radiance Prenatal Process, which takes place in water heated to the temperature of the womb. The process is always conducted by a male-female team.

The process begins with a discussion of the client's prenatal experience, investigating stressors such as cigarette and alcohol consumption by the mother, deep emotions which may have been transmitted to the child in utero, whether he or she was unwanted or unloved, and other relevant background information. The client is then invited to relax in the water while being supported by the therapists. There is an induction process which takes the client back to the prenatal time. When the person is engaged, the therapists carry out a clearing procedure to free the person from any troublesome feelings that may have been experienced prenatally and to replace negative self-esteem with a clear sense of being loved and wanted. Then, direct work on the person's body frees tension and postural quirks, particularly from the head, neck and shoulders. At the end of the session most people are profoundly relaxed. In fact, the last fifteen minutes of the process are devoted to preparing the person to handle gravity again.

We have asked clients who have gone through the process to fill out a brief questionnaire. From the self-reports we have received, four common themes have emerged: postural changes, a deepened experience of love, a sense of connection to self, and a deeper feeling of belonging here.

Most postural changes have involved the spine. One woman reported a "permanent change, especially in the relationship of head and neck to trunk." Another person reported that the process had permanently corrected a spinal problem which had been treated with chiropractic manipulation for years. A man reported the disappearance of his "little-boy stance," a pelvis-retracted, belly-out posture. For another person, a long-term neck pain, which had not yielded to a number of bodywork modalities, cleared up.

Many clients reported a bodily feeling of love which was new and profoundly different. Among the comments we have received are:

"My body, at a cellular level, knows that it has experienced being loved."

"I feel the essence of who I am was touched and loved."

"The experience of love entering my belly started a roll, giving me momentum and the memory of love and support to remain open to deep feelings daily over a period of weeks."

The sense of connection with self was summarized by a young woman. "The general figure-ground that I experience myself in is more peaceful and grounded. I now look more to my core for confirmation than to the outside with other people."

One of the primary goals in prenatal work is to provide a context where the client can deeply experience a sense of belonging in the world. This experience was most clearly expressed in the following report:

> And so what I got a glimpse of, and can recall by memory, is that I am welcome here. I don't recall it often, but when I do I well up with tears. That was not in my experience previously.

Many of the phenomena that emerge when the person is reliving birth, prenatal or conception events have to be seen to be believed. In fact, we ourselves had a hard time believing them when we first started experiencing them in ourselves and seeing them in our clients. Now with two decades of experience, our minds have had a chance to catch up with our bodies, and we have developed a theoretical structure which makes sense of the appearance of these earlier events during therapy. The techniques we use, whether breath, movement, sound or the more spiritual aspects like love and awareness, all seem to have a cellular effect. A change to deeper breathing, for example, affects every cell in the body within seconds. Sound vibrates the whole body; attention can be measured scientifically to have a cellular effect. So it stands to reason that these techniques can awaken cellular memory. It also makes sense that we have a cellular memory of the events of our lives, recorded as on a big computer. This recording of cellular memory would seem to be required for evolution to proceed. An example: many times we have seen forceps marks appear on the head of someone who is reliving birth trauma. Then, as quickly, the marks disappear. How can this be? Where have the marks been all this time? The only explanation we can offer is through the mechanisms of cellular memory, awakened by a breath or an awareness decades later. In our training we show many videos of these events, which are not easily described through words. If you are drawn to an exploration of these early events in your life and in the lives of your clients, we would welcome you at one of our brief workshops or longer trainings, so that you can see birth, prenatal and conception with your own eyes.

CHAPTER FIVE

Radiance Movement Therapy

Dorothy came into the session in obvious distress. She said her right side felt "crushed," and she had a bad headache. In fact, her right eyelid was drooping, and the right side of her face looked as if it were melting. What really drew my attention, though, was her left upper lip, which curled into a snarl when she talked. I (KH) asked her to turn her attention to her lip and to breathe into that area. As she began to close her eyes and focus on her lip I added, "Let yourself open up to the way your lip wants to move. Follow that." She began to curl her lip up until her cheek started trembling. I encouraged her to continue letting her lip lead more and more movement of her body, as I mentioned shoulders, ribs, and hands.

Her middle-aged face began to dissolve into the face of an infant as she allowed her body to list to the right and finally collapse on the floor. Her mouth began bubbling, and she cried and mewed as her hands curled up around her face. I held her head and lower back very lightly as I murmured to her, "Go deeply into that place. Find out what's there for you." I matched her breathing, and she suddenly began deep sobbing and rocking. After several minutes her body relaxed into the floor, and she became quite still for a while. She took a deep breath finally and said she felt "exhausted, but clear." She felt in touch with her right side, and her headache was gone.

Each person has his or her own journey and purpose. In Radiance Movement Therapy we use a process to open up the meaning in everyday movements such as walking or starting and stopping. The key to more aliveness and wholeness lies within these simple movements. In this chapter I would like to explore the nature of movement, its language, and the process by which it can be mobilized for liberation.

It is truly astounding to realize how intimately and exactly our bodies reflect our relationship to life. The play of personality flickers over our unique gestures and ripples through the movements we repeat again and again. The man who feels his shoulders draw in realizes he's frightened in new situations. The woman who periodically trips and bumps into things discovers she feels unsure of the next step in her life at these times. The woman who bustles everywhere at top speed feels her sadness when she slows down. The man who discovers spinning and whirling sees how much he likes to expand into new areas.

Beneath the surface play of personality we each experience the need to feel whole. Movement that is united lights up our insides and reminds us that we can become more. Movement can connect us directly with our innermost being. It can also reflect the cloak of roles we wear to disguise our needs and feelings.

The basic rhythm of life is expansion and contraction, reaching out to embrace life and contracting to find our own center again. The expanding and contracting cycles of our bodies include breathing, sleeping and waking, and striding out to work and retreating to rest. Everything pulsates in this rhythm. Because we are conscious beings, we can choose how we respond to this basic pulsation. When we can accept and participate with the ebb and flow, life goes smoothly. When we resist, edit and withdraw from the insistance of this biological pulsation, we lose touch with ourselves and the universe around us. As we grow up most of us learn to resist.

Through repeated experience, most of us have learned to see the body as a thing. We think that the body's main purpose is to support the head (e.g., "The chief function of your body is to carry your brain around"—Thomas Edison). We are taught that the body is not quite good enough and needs to be severely constrained and conditioned to operate efficiently. By example we begin to suspect that our bodies and impulses are dangerous and unpredictable. No wonder we gradually stop participating in the great breath of life. For example, one client currently experiencing a painful mid-life transition describes herself as "the" body or "the" arms, as in, "The body has been feeling okay this week." She is just beginning to understand how clearly her words reflect her alienation from herself.

Each breath provides the opportunity to participate with—or withdraw from—that moment's feelings and needs. Withdrawal creates a particular template in the neuromuscular system that, over time, can be seen in the distortions, contracted muscles, repeated mannerisms and movement patterns which we call character and use to identify ourselves and each other.

The Persona Principle

*W*e see the personality when we see a person move. The dart of an eye or the hunch of a shoulder broadcasts our beliefs, self-concepts, social conditioning, needs and issues. In short, how we move is who we are. For example, in a hospital in-service training I asked the therapists to choose one patient on the unit to observe.

The therapist was to observe the patient's walk enough to be able to duplicate it for the training group. One therapist came in who had observed an adolescent boy and had practiced taking on his walk. As she walked for the group we all noticed two distinct personalities. One was very fast, leading from her upper torso, and almost looked like an animal sniffing out his prey. The other walk was a modified "trucking" walk with her upper torso held back and her body bouncing along heel to heel. In the discussion, the therapist's key comment was her surprise at how exactly this boy's walk matched the way he was on the unit. She said he was "either totally spaced out and bumping into things or getting his nose in everybody's business." In both walks the central issue was the lack of boundaries in contacting others.

The major task of Radiance Movement Therapy is to assist clients to reclaim their direct connection with life—their full aliveness. Many years ago when I was training to become a dance/movement therapist, I noticed that there was a visible difference between just going through the motions and an electric quality that was only present when the mover and the movement became one. I began to explore what could make such a dramatic difference and if that quality of authenticity could be nurtured and taught. My growing conviction is that intention and attention are the keys to transformation through the body. I've seen that motion without conscious intention, whatever its form or purpose, changes only the outer layers of the personality, one's character and coping style.

Intention

*I*ntention creates the context for movement. One's deepest intentions and original decisions shape movement. A primary intention to prove that you're good enough will shape a very different physical form than the intention to get even. Intention creates the body we experience. In movement therapy we examine old unconscious intentions and create new conscious ones that will serve the highest purpose of the individual. Setting intentions within the movement session strips movement of baroque flourishes, drama, and layers of repetition. The movement process itself becomes simpler and clearer until we finally touch our essence. For example, an intention to clear up whatever obstacles prevent a direct relationship with oneself and the universe will create the context for the movement to take away the veil of illusion from one's senses until an unmistakably vital relationship emerges. Along the way the incomplete past experiences and moments of unconsciousness emerge in the mover's awareness and can be embraced and dissolved.

To illustrate this principle, I'll describe a portion of a recent movement session. While exploring a strong pattern of tucking in his chin over a collapsed chest, the client realized that his intention in that movement sequence and its matching emotional state was to "stonewall" and not show any response to an abusive parent. The intention had generalized so strongly that he had difficulty being vulnerable, especially with woman, even when he wished. He decided to consciously alter his intention to be permeable to his own feelings and to others and was then able to fluff and fill out his chin and to soften his contact. He began to directly sense the feminine in himself.

The Basic Practice

*T*he central methodology in Radiance Movement Therapy is the focus on process. I begin by having the client tune in to whatever he or she is experiencing. In *The Secret of the Golden Flower* the practice of focused attention is introduced by the phrase "circulate the light backwards." Within the movement context, I understand this phrase to mean, take the attention that you habitually turn outward to the world and focus it inward. The decision to turn the light of attention inward has great power to illuminate complex inner structures and patterns and to actually transform them. In this central practice the intention is to follow, witness and participate with internal sensation. The mover is repeatedly invited to ATTEND INWARDLY, EXPERIENCE FULLY, AND EXPRESS IN MOVEMENT WHAT SHE OR HE IS EXPERIENCING.

In the third session with a new client, I asked how she was feeling. She quickly said "Fine." I responded that her body didn't seem to match "fine," and I asked her to turn her attention to any tense areas in her body with the intention of experiencing whatever was needed. After about ten seconds she opened her eyes sharply and tears were visibly welling up in her eyes. I asked her what she noticed and she mentioned tension in her shoulders, not her tearing. I gently brought her attention to her tears, and her face began to pucker as she tried not to cry. I asked her to find out how she was stopping herself from crying, and she replied she was holding her breath and distracting herself mentally. As she was saying this more tears welled up behind her eyes. When asked to breathe into her face and ride along on the impulse, she cried openly while wringing her hands and said she could sense how the wave of feeling arose at intervals. She became involved in that cycle, and we spent the whole session turning attention inward, experiencing sadness and allowing expression. She became aware of unexperienced grief over her sister's death and the rhythm of mourning that had been pushing her for years.

The quality of attention that allows the light of awareness to circulate inwards includes a willingness to release the interference of the conditioned mind. It is very close to what in Zen is called bare attention. A great deal of the initial work in movement teaches clients to notice just what is happening as they move, nothing extra. So much of our conditioning has emphasized doing it right, fulfilling roles or avoiding embarrassing loss of face, that the initial request to pay attention to oneself meets an army of shoulds, shouldn'ts and ought to's. One often hears, "This is just how I am," or "Why do I do that?"

The healing attitude is to inquire into the CONTEXT AND PATTERN, rather than the specific content with all its baggage. For example, a young woman in a long-term, good relationship found herself suddenly consumed by a crush on another man. She judged herself and made resolutions and felt bewildered. Instead of engaging with her at that level I asked her to focus on how her body reflected the feelings she was experiencing. As she focused inward she realized that "feeling bad" was always followed by a grin, that she actually felt energized in some way by creating a situation in which to "feel bad." Continuing to explore the pattern in movement, she discovered that "feeling bad" was a way she kept herself grounded when things were going too well for her to handle. We could then explore several alternatives to ground her that were more convenient: leaping and whooping to celebrate her energy or moving and breathing more when the grin emerged.

The Basic Paradigm

On the way to the core, we journey through three layers. The outer layer, Level One in Illustration 1 (page 56), represents the social shell we've built as a result of our conditioning. This shell is our everyday movement. In beginning movement therapy we work with the basic parameters of movement: walking, making transitions, moving fast and slow, up and down, and starting and stopping. Our intention is to illuminate the habitual patterns of responding to the world. Level Two represents the unconscious patterns that may arise in dreams or body sensations and dis-ease. Level Two contains the parts of ourselves we've disowned and tend to project onto others. Level Three, which is directly wrapped around and covering our core life-energy, is the deepest belief which Levels One and Two reflect and anchor. The movement cycle is complete when the underlying belief has been directly experienced throughout the bodymind.

To illustrate this basic paradigm, let's go through a client's session, pictured in Illustration 2 (page 57). Terry could be described as a triple type-A: efficient, very quick, socially skilled (Level One), and terrified of her insides. When she came into a recent session, she said she had noticed a strong and painful pulling on her right midsection, as if "it really wanted to scrunch down" (Level Two). She had felt really stuck in that sensation for the last week. I asked her to lie down and breathe into her right side. I suggested that she move from the inside out, listening very carefully to what her right side had to say. Within just two minutes she allowed her

Level One:
    The Mask
    Body Armor
    Repetitive Kinetic Patterns

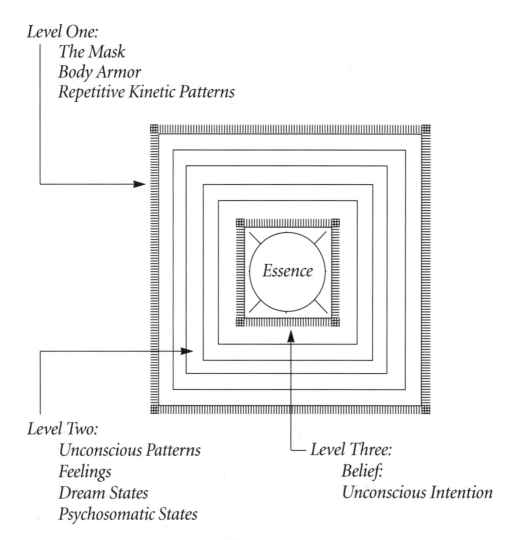

Level Two:
    Unconscious Patterns   *Level Three:*
    Feelings   *Belief:*
    Dream States   *Unconscious Intention*
    Psychosomatic States

Illustration One

movement to take over, and she looked as if she were trying to get out of something. Her body twitched powerfully, and her movements were sharp and striking out, almost like a convulsion. The phrase that seemed to fit was, "Don't you touch me!" She moved spontaneously for about twenty-five minutes, and her body became very hot and sweaty. Part way through the sequence, she got up very suddenly and began taking the same level of intensity into standing movement. She said the movement felt like, "If you won't love me, I won't, I just won't, I won't play!" (Level Three). With the words came anguished tears for several minutes. When they subsided, Terry had several insights about her early experience that had led her to the decision to "not play." The pain in her right side was gone, and she continued to need to move a lot over the next few days as more connections emerged.

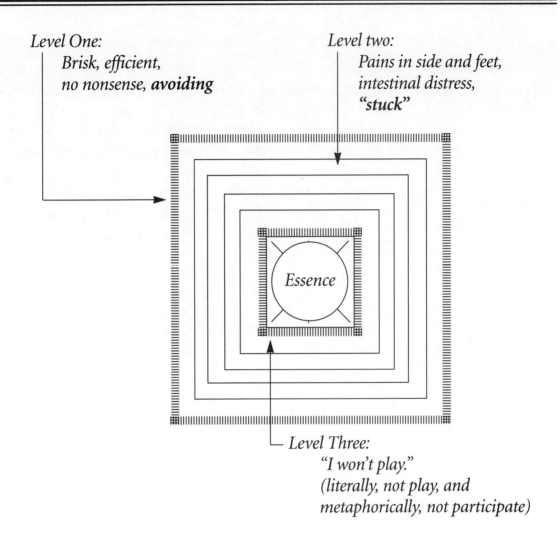

Level One:
  Brisk, efficient,
  no nonsense, **avoiding**

Level two:
  Pains in side and feet,
  intestinal distress,
  "stuck"

Essence

Level Three:
  "I won't play."
  (literally, not play, and
  metaphorically, not participate)

Illustration Two

Process Components

GOING WITH is a phrase I repeat often in sessions. To go with is to befriend that impulse, that unacknowledged part. Over and over, I learn that resistance is the only problem. All impulses and feelings can be experienced. Going with is FOLLOWING WHAT MOST DEEPLY WANTS TO HAPPEN. The intention is to open up to the impulse as it is, not as it should be or might be if it were improved. Useful verbalizations that facilitate going with are:

"What wants to happen here?"
"Give yourself permission to open fully to that impulse."

"Breathe into that place and follow the sensation with your hands."
"Open up to that just as it is."

I was working with a woman who carried most of her weight in her buttocks and thighs. I asked her to walk and noticed a strong backward pull that centered in her low back and buttocks. When I brought it to her attention and asked her to go with that pull, she initially felt frightened by it and kept trying to forge through forward space. But once noticed, that backward pull became stronger. When she went with the pull and let it direct her movement, she realized that her hip and thigh area was her internalized critical mother, the part of her that held her back from her full potential, and that kept her from going further than her mother had gone. In the previous year, as she entered graduate school, her buttocks became large; she had more backaches; and she had to try harder to keep moving forward.

ATTENTION IS DIRECTED TO BODILY EXPERIENCE. The body is the treasure chest, and Pandora's box, of stored incomplete experiences, memories, faulty solutions to problems, attitudes, and conditioned responses. One of human beings' most common defenses against this seeming chaos of the body is to intellectualize in one way or another. The question, "How are you experiencing that in your body?" is repeated frequently, especially in the beginning phase of the movement work. As we return again and again to the body we get acquainted. We learn about who we actually are. Involvement increases with the cycle of going inward, experiencing and expressing. When involvement expands to a certain point, an experiential shift may occur in one of the following ways:

1. A memory arises and is connected to current issues.

2. There is suddenly more internal space.

3. A feeling is fully released.

4. Perception expands and the world looks cleaner, more beautiful.

5. A breath moves through like a big bubble to a sigh, chuckle, or exclamation.

Some phrases that assist body involvement are:

"Let yourself be nervous (or heavy, or pulled, or whatever the visible state is)."
"When you do that, notice what happens to the rest of your body."
"Where do you feel that most in your body?"
"Gradually let all of you become that quality (the pressure in the chest, the contraction in the stomach, whatever the sensation is)."
"Breathe into that as you move."

GOING DEEPER is an essential direction of the work. This is in contrast to the habitual tendency to try to get away from or to get rid of the issue. The possibility of going deeper depends on the environment, the therapist's attitudes, and a certain structure. A sense of safety seems to be necessary in order to create a container for the inner confusion and chaos to bounce against. Safety of place and relationship assists the client to more easily reach the unconscious and bring it to light.

I put a great deal of time and awareness into the physical environment where the work takes place. My working environment invites comfort and symbolic association. I use a large, empty, open space. The pictures and hangings on the wall suggest movement, interior journeys, and slowing down. The colors are bright and warm-hued, and the room contains both formal furniture and many pillows which can be arranged for sitting on a rug.

Clients are invited to actively explore the space in the first few sessions. One initial question I ask is, "What do you need in order to make this a safe space for you?" I have many props and materials for creating environments (cloths, blocks, costumes, etc.), and often clients will build a safe space and remain inside for some time. The acknowledgement of this need seems basic to subsequent work. In addition to or instead of building a physical safe space, clients will sometimes create an imaginary environment around themselves. I invite this movement fantasy by asking, "If you close your eyes and imagine a comfortable container around your body, what does it look like? As you explore and feel with your body, what do you notice about this container? Does it have thick walls? Is it transparent or solid, etc.?" I ask clients to keep exploring until they feel at home in this container, then I will ask them to slowly open their eyes and move about the room taking their container with them.

So many people have chosen to protect themselves by becoming rigid and narrow that the therapy alliance seems to require new, more flexible defenses before deeper exploration can occur. Sometimes people will feel safest in a particular area of the room, or seated on a special pillow, or with eyes initially closed. Clients begin to take charge of their work with these anchors.

In the movement work itself, matching qualities seems to allow the work to deepen and to allow direct access to Levels Two and Three. To suggest, "Let your breath support your movement," often brings a brand new sensation to awareness. The intention is to bring the client's awareness into congruence with underlying impulses. For example, a possible suggestion is, "Allow as much insistence in that walk as you're feeling." In deepening, we want to explore WHAT IS, not what the client has been trying to project. A person's awareness will easily slip to a deeper level when the internal awareness and external movement match.

As the movement work progresses, the client is encouraged to continue trusting a growing internal sense of correct pacing as unknown issues and new psychological territory unfold. A common suggestion here is, "Spend a few minutes letting your body tell you what it needs to feel safe in this particular situation."

The therapist uses her or his attention in the process of going deeper to notice distractions and tangential movement, and to reflect them to the client. The therapist interrupts "automatic" movement that releases tension but detracts from the issue. Legs often take on this function with pacing or shuffling. I will gently remind clients to only move their legs if their deepest impulses direct them. Verbal questions which invite deepening are often useful, such as:

"Would you let yourself go down into that?"
"What is that movement saying to you?"
"What is underneath (or around) that sensation?"

When deepening is invited, as when the pebble settles in the pond, two kinds of ripples are generated. Layers of resistance are encountered (Level Two), and obstacles emerge as part of the transition between levels. In the Radiance Movement Therapy process these OBSTACLES ARE ACKNOWLEDGED AND EXPLORED as legitimate voices and parts of the whole person. Content is not valued as much as the client's PARTICIPATION with experience and expression. The therapist can learn to see emerging movement obstacles. Some of the signs that an obstacle has emerged are: solidity, immovability, density of tissues, and unvaried contraction. The key to opening the obstacle often lies, quite literally, underneath or behind or around the apparent obstacle. As the client explores the qualities of the obstacle, the context and driving attitudes (Level Three) anchoring the obstacle often come to immediate awareness. The methodology for exploring an obstacle includes breathing into it, letting its feeling quality expand to include greater body involvement (e.g., allowing the hands and arms to move as the quality of a stomach pain), and most importantly, being with it.

For example, in a session with a young college student who had many unresolved family issues, I noticed that her left hand kept shaping itself into a claw-like crippled form. I encouraged her to expand this shape by allowing her arm, shoulder, and then her torso to also carry and move that particular quality and sensation. As she moved she began to have feelings about and images of her mother. I noticed that her right side became more massive and blocky as she attended to her left side, so I suggested that she begin to let left and right sides dialogue in movement. I encouraged her to pace her movement from the actual body signal, expressing right and left sides as rapidly as the impulse arose. Her movement almost immediately dropped any superfluous gesturing, and she swung between her right hand and her voice saying, "I'll get you! Just you wait!" to her left hand and side sniveling, retreating, and enduring passively. This spontaneous combustion lasted several frenetic, escalating minutes until she seemed to pop through into an "aha!" realization. She understood all at once how she had unconsciously internalized the conflict between her father and mother, making it her problem and her responsibility to resolve the issues that had divided her family. That movement sequence was an important step in her individuation process.

A cycle of dissolving and reforming may occur once or several times in the course of the work. This cycle can occur in daily life as the work deepens, and it can occur each session if Level Three is opening. Old patterns and automatic responses begin to feel uncomfortable to the client as increased awareness makes them more conscious. At this juncture the client rarely knows what he or she REALLY wants or what the issue REALLY is. Nothing seems to fit, and the client may feel and say that "everything is falling apart."

This is the impasse, THE obstacle. It signals that the client's habitual way of responding no longer works. The mask has cracked, but the new way of being has not been established yet. The impasse occurs just before the client breaks through the death layer into a deeper relationship with life energy.

Signals that the impasse has been reached include:

1. The client gets sick, often with an illness that has occurred periodically throughout life.

2. The client shuts down sensory awareness and responds to inquiries with shrugs, sighs and the phrase, "I don't know."

3. The client expresses despair that things will NEVER change.

4. The client experiences in life an increase of things actually falling apart, either at the level of toasters and cars or his or her body.

5. The client wants to quit, to have life go back to the way it was.

6. The client gets angry at the therapist and says or feels it's the therapist's fault for getting him or her into this mess. For example, the client may say, "I've faithfully done everything you asked me to do, and I just feel worse."

In any given session the client may hit an impasse, that place between the resolution of an old pattern and the birth of a new mode of behavior. The client's awareness actually implodes in this experience, and it creates a density in the environment in which the therapist can get caught. When the impasse occurs, the therapist often:

1. finds his or her mind wandering;

2. feels sleepy (REALLY sleepy, as if being dragged down);

3. is drawn into the sense of hopelessness;

4. feels stymied and ineffective;

5. notices greatly increased heaviness in his or her breathing and body awareness.

Dealing with this state is one of the more delicate tasks in the work. Once an impasse is suspected, the therapist can begin to assist movement using the basic tools of process work. The therapist's awareness and experience that this impasse is normal and not the end of the road can help unfold the implosion for the client. For example, in a recent session Angela came in, sat hunched over without saying anything, and looked at me from under her eyebrows with a half-smirk, half-frown. Her body looked bloated and strained. I asked her how the week had gone, and she said she felt she must not be cut out for motherhood. Her infant son had been waking up several times during the night for weeks, and she was just frazzled. "He's just always there," she exclaimed. She felt as if she "whined" all the time, which she "couldn't stand!" She just felt stuck, she said, as she shrugged her shoulders.

I noticed myself wondering if she really might have an impossible situation here, and felt my own internal process turn sluggish. I wondered how we would get through this hour, as I glanced at the clock. Then I realized we were probably in an impasse.

So I asked her to exaggerate the whining in sounds and movement. She sat on the floor rocking, scuttling, and making small hand movements. Suddenly she stopped and said, "This is ridiculous!" I asked her to explore her feeling of "ridiculous" and what she actually experienced with that word. She noticed she would hold her breath and actually freeze her body movement, as if someone had grabbed and pushed her shoulders. I invited her to repeat that response several times while noticing what was underneath the experience of "ridiculous" in her body. She quickly noticed (and I felt) her sadness, although she didn't know what it was about.

I asked her to let her body dialogue with "ridiculous" and "sad." As she moved she realized that SHE wanted to be taken care of. I asked if she would like to be held. She was a little shy but agreed to lay her head on my lap. While I stroked her hair lightly and paid attention to her, she lay very quietly. After some time she said, "What a relief it is not to have to respond." When she sat back up she looked refreshed and relaxed. Her voice had dropped the whine. She and I spent the remaining minutes brainstorming other ways she could be taken care of: time away, a massage, hot baths, etc.

Body armor, an aspect of Level One, is a specific type of obstacle that comes to awareness in the movement process. The client is invited to befriend unowned areas rather than repressing or denying any aspect of the self. The client's willingness to solve the problem is especially useful with chronically tense, rigid or unmoving parts of the body. Willingness allows a more gentle approach than do classic bioenergetic stress postures or the perspective that a pitched battle is occurring. The possibility of new options, a next step, opens up when the underlying integrative drive of seemingly ineffective behavior or structure is recognized.

There are several specific aspects of working with body armor that have been useful. I often ask clients to use the movement of their breath in combination with the focus of their attention to gently loosen armor. For example, with facial and mouth tensions, I may suggest, "Let the breath move up behind your mouth and gently bring new sensations to your awareness." Another technique is to shift one's perspective while in the stuck place, as in the suggestion, "Move from the inside out into the space around you." That shift will often loosen the logjam and tangibly expand the client's perceived boundaries. Clients are also asked to notice where an impulse might move through the body if they weren't fixating it. For example, "Where might your hands move if you weren't clenching them?" Or, "How would your chest move if you let go of the breath instead of holding it up high under your shoulders?" Another valuable method is to direct the client to move and breathe at the same time. This may seem obvious, but most often people equate movement with effort and have already established a habit of holding the breath when efforting. I will usually suggest that the breath be allowed to support the movement, as that suggestion allows optimal client responsibility.

Another kind of obstacle to individuation and the experience of wholeness is repetition of specific movement patterns. I have frequently heard, in classes or with clients, the uncomfortable admission, "I find myself coming back to the same movement over and over." Sometimes people will freeze at this point and feel they've "run out" of new movement. Since the concern here is not to create a performance but to contact directly the obstacles to a free flow of experience and expression, these moments of repetition and paralysis are quite valuable.

Repetitive movement patterns contain clues to unfinished experiences from the client's past and are excellent doors into Level Three awareness. Repetitive movement patterns are pictures of arrested emotional states. They are almost like dreams in that they condense symbolic meaning and feeling in apparently simple movements. Patterns that are useful to follow will generally have a charged quality, a sense that you've stumbled onto a secret. I look for individual mannerisms such as hair twirling, finger flicking or head tilting, as well as repetitive qualities like circling motions, constant unvaried slowness or a sense of weight pulling downward. Amplifying these patterns and attending very closely to the total body response to inquiry, can unearth the unfinished business and free the unconscious compulsion to return to the pattern.

For example, one client presented an unvarying and very pronounced body lean to the right when sitting or standing. The image of her that I pictured was of an infant whose head is still too heavy for the undeveloped neck muscles to support. The heaviness flopped her head over to the right, compressing her whole side. We explored lifting and dropping her head, peering out at the world from the back-in-there space of that body attitude, and other amplifications as we sat together.

I asked her to stand then and let the heaviness and pull become even greater, to see where it wanted to take her in space. As she moved, a spiral shape emerged that seemed to expand her comfort in moving. She suddenly recalled her last night's dream, in which her insides were a prison and outside was a raging war.

On the heels of recounting this dream she became aware of a deep suspicion she had toward her right side which made her right-led movement very indirect and spiralling. I designated a pillow in the room to represent her right side and asked her to approach it and then move away from it very directly in the suspicious, spiralling way. First she took a long time moving indirectly toward the pillow, which was her more familiar style. When she moved toward the object directly, her movement became very heavy and slow. She began talking to the object as if it were her alcoholic father. She saw him as a corpse, and realized she had been carrying him around (on her right side) and felt responsible for him and his well-being. That realization brought a flood of feeling, tears and angry flailing. After a little, she began to understand that she had chosen that response to a very difficult home life, and could choose a new response.

Putting It Together

*T*he methodology of working with repetitive patterns illustrates the basic paradigm, since all unconsicous conflicts will repeat themselves in an attempt to come to completion. The overall goal is to make the deepest unconscious belief conscious throughout the body so that the Level Three attitudes cease to run the system. When this occurs the person can make new choices that emanate from his or her essential nature.

The first important step is to draw attention to the pattern(s), Level One, as most people are totally unaware of them. Here are some ways that lead to deeper awareness of a pattern:

1. Use videotape feedback.

2. Ask, "Is this familiar?"

3. Suggest, "Become aware of what you're doing here."

Be prepared for defensive responses such as "That's just the way I am!" Defensive responses indicate a need to explore issues of safety.

The next step is to uncover Level Two. Here the basic cycle of turning inward, experiencing, and expressing in movement is taught. Skill with this cycle builds a bridge between mind and body, conscious and unconscious. Helpful tools for this step include the following:

1. Interrupt distracting movements.

2. Create a metaphor for the intangible aspect of the movement from your intuitive sense.

3. Invite the person to follow what wants to happen as he or she focuses on body sensations.

The door to Level Three is often opened by exploring polarities. In the example of the woman with the right-sided lean, the biggest shift occurred when I asked her to approach the object directly AND indirectly. The woman whose hand was clenched had her "aha!" realization after dialoguing with her left AND right hands. Most clients are stuck in either-or choices and responses that bind the repetitive pattern and create a sense of futility about change. AND instead of or and BOTH instead of either can bridge opposites and allow a new synthesis to occur.

A crucial question can be asked which will uncover the belief structure and its tentacles. A general form of this question is, "Would you be willing to go all the way with this issue (feeling, pattern) and clear it up so that it doesn't bother you any more?" The timing of this question is delicate. The mover needs to be experiencing Level Two patterns in an expanded state of awareness. If it's asked too soon the mover has no experiential sense of the issue. If it's asked too late the door has closed, and the mover's awareness has returned to Level One.

An affirmative response to this question seems to open space for the underlying belief to rise into awareness. The belief or attitude holds all other levels in place. When it dissolves, the pattern ceases. Confusion and dizziness can emerge when the belief structure is dissolving, as can the deepest fears of death and craziness. This alchemical moment is created and held by a safe environment, trust in the therapeutic relationship, the therapist's deep experience of death and rebirth, and the context of love and allowing in which all the work takes place. Beyond belief is clear life energy, free energy that wants to play and create and celebrate.

The mover's body knows how long to stay at this level and will close the door quite naturally at the internal signal—enough for now. The therapist can best serve by holding the mover in loving awareness and by witnessing the unfolding. No other help is needed. As the cycle completes, the outer layers of the body structure will reform DIFFERENTLY. The person will move and feel differently and may take a while to feel fully in touch with the ground and the environment again.

Clarification and expression are valuable grounding tools after the client has completed a movement cycle. If the movement cycle doesn't reach resolution through Level Three, suggestions at the end of the session are focused on connecting the movement experience to daily life. Some examples of questions follow.

1. How is this pattern familiar?

2. When do you notice yourself, for example, getting smaller?

3. When you are aware of this pattern, do you see any alternative?

4. Would you be willing to allow this pattern to dissolve as you go about your day-to-day life?

I want the client to take charge of completing the integration of the experience. As he integrated his session, one client wrote the following poem:

> DANCE to the urge eternal
> DANCE to the pull from the sky
> DANCE with others beside you
> DANCE to the internal aye!
> DANCE through the cracks in the armor
> DANCE where the opening goes
> DANCE to the beat of the cosmos
> DANCE being pulled by your toes!
> DANCE knowing you are a dancer
> DANCE like a finch in the air
> DANCE when you're not in a good space
> DANCE where your friends wouldn't dare
> DANCE to Orion
> DANCE to the grass
> DANCE with your future
> DANCE with your past
> DANCE in your heart, and
> DANCE with your breath
> DANCE to your birthday, and
> DANCE to your death.
> —Ron Noel

CHAPTER SIX

The Bodymind Centering Techniques

Introduction

Bodymind Centering is a precise, step-by-step technique for solving life problems through contact with the Inner Self. With Bodymind Centering, you enter a relaxed state, then follow a series of clear, simple steps. You apply Bodymind Centering to any problem or issue that interests you. People have used the technique to heal mental, physical, emotional and relationship problems.

The essence of change is the act of making contact with your Inner Self. In the thirty years or more that the authors have practiced psychotherapy, it has become clear to us that true happiness comes from having a congenial relationship between Inner Self and Outer Self. To be with people as they make this contact is one of the richest, most satisfying experiences life has to offer.

A 45-year-old woman discovered that her near-daily headaches were her body's way of saying, "I'm angry and I don't know what to do about it." She found a more direct way of expressing her anger, and her headaches ceased. A man, 50, used Bodymind Centering to find out why he engaged in numerous infidelities despite his love for his wife. He discovered that his affairs were a way of convincing himself that he was youthful and immortal. His Inner Self knew the answer, and was just waiting to be asked.

Until recently, psychology had few reliable tools for contacting the Inner Self, and most of those tools required the services of a professional. Although it was proverbial that the answers lay inside ourselves, there were few reliable maps of the territory or navigational devices. Bodymind Centering is both a map and a technology for finding your way through the inner world. It has been used on every problem people are likely to face, from backaches to phobias to relationship conflicts.

Bodymind Centering can be incorporated into a variety of clinical practices, from counseling to massage therapy, as well as educational settings. Its gentle approach makes it an ideal introduction to transformational work. Most people come in with two basic complaints: "I don't know what I feel" and "I don't know how to express myself." The experience of Bodymind Centering connects us tangibly to our inner resources and makes a bridge to their expression.

It is unfortunate that formal schooling, with its thousands of hours devoted to math and science, often does not spend a minute teaching us how to go within, to find out who we are, to deal with our deeper feelings, or to heal the rift between Outer Self and Inner Self. It is up to us to do it ourselves. We must take up the challenge and face, with the courage of Columbus, the profoundly rewarding vistas within ourselves.

Why and How Bodymind Centering Works

*I*n the process of growing up, most of us develop two distinct selves. The first, which we will call the Inner Self (IS, pronounced like the verb "is"), contains all our original, primary reactions to things. Some examples of IS are joy, anger, fear, sexual feelings, and hunger.

Later in our development, we assemble an Outer Self (OS, pronounced as in Wizard of Oz). OS is made up of what is socially acceptable in our particular environment.

The Inner Selves of human beings are remarkably similar; the Outer Selves are remarkably varied. This is because what works in one family may be utterly different from what works in the family next door. For example, one child may learn that a temper tantrum works as a way of expressing anger in one family. In the family next door, another child may learn to hold in the anger and turn it into a headache.

If you are fortunate, you will grow up with a friendly relationship between IS and OS. In other words, there will not be a large gap between how you feel on the inside and how you act on the outside. For example, you feel tension in your shoulders. You look inside yourself and realize, "Oh, I'm tightening my shoulders because I'm afraid of that conversation I have to have with my boss today."

Unfortunately, many of us have been living in OS for so long that we have lost touch with IS. We have been so busy protecting our Inner Self and assembling more complex layers of OS, that we have lost touch with IS. So IS must speak to us sharply, through the language of the body: pain, tension, conflict, or illness. The Inner Self becomes buried under a pile of decisions to ignore it.

How Bodymind Centering Came To Be

Early in the authors' careers as therapists, we noticed that people's lives really started changing when they got in contact with the Inner Self. It was the act of contact that brought about rapid movement, not so much what they contacted. For example, a man came in one day and excitedly reported a dream with a green light in it. He had asked himself what the green light meant, and a surprisingly meaningful answer had come back in a flash. His Inner Self told him that the green light meant he should go ahead on a certain real estate project. It was his first experience with getting information directly from IS, and it signalled a major turning point in his life.

These "aha!" experiences are often life-changing; they are signals that your Inner and Outer Selves are back in harmony with each other. Bodymind Centering is effective, even if you do not have "aha!" experiences right away. To understand why this is so, we will describe the inner workings of Bodymind Centering.

At first, you will do Bodymind Centering seated with eyes closed. Later, as your skills increase, you will learn how to do it in movement and in daily life. You begin by going through several steps to relax your body and get in touch with IS. Then you select an issue or problem to work on. You ask questions of your Inner Self, and you listen for answers. The answers may be words, pictures, or even body sensations. You continue as long as you find it meaningful and enjoyable. Then you return to normal activity. The process takes fifteen to twenty minutes in your initial practice. Once you have a feel for the basic process, you can do it for a few seconds or an hour.

Bodymind Centering works because it sets up a new relationship between IS and OS. In most of us, the Outer Self is boss. It tells the Inner Self how and what to feel. Naturally, this relationship is not very productive and results in pain, tension, and conflict. With Bodymind Centering, the Outer Self learns to listen to the Inner Self, and herein lies the "magic" of the technique. By setting up a relationship between equals, the two selves gradually come into harmony with each other. Rapid change is often the result, even if the person does not have "aha!" experiences while doing Bodymind Centering.

With an understanding now of how and why Bodymind Centering works, let us find out some of the things you are likely to discover as you explore the inner world.

What's in There?

*A*s you explore the inner world using Bodymind Centering, you are bound to discover things you did not know about yourself. Based on the experiences of many people who have used Bodymind Centering, the authors have collected thousands of examples of life-changing discoveries. In this section, we have sorted these experiences into several main categories with examples of each. Your experience with Bodymind Centering will of course be unique, but it may contain some of the following insights and discoveries.

FEELINGS

One of the major insights you may have with Bodymind Centering is the discovery of feelings you did not know you were feeling. Human beings are often quick to cover their real feelings, often so quickly that we do not realize we have felt a particular feeling.

Anger. One of the major feelings humans hide is anger. It is easy to see why we hide it: We've been punished for being angry. So we hide it to protect our hides.

Ellen, a successful banker in her mid-forties, had been experiencing hives since she was a child. Suddenly, for no reason she could discern, she would break out in an "angry" rash. Using Bodymind Centering, she explored the feelings and sensations that went along with the hives. The first few times she used Bodymind Centering she did not feel that it helped. The experience was relaxing and pleasant, but it did not yield any substantial results. On her fourth Bodymind Centering she struck gold. She discovered that her hives always followed incidents where she felt anger but did not express it to the person at whom she was angry. The hives were her body's way of saying, "I'm angry." Ellen did not stop there. She kept using Bodymind Centering until she came up with a creative way of dealing with anger. Instead of hiding the anger, she allowed the sensations of anger to flow through her entire body. Then, if she felt the person could handle it, she would express the anger to them. Over the next few months her hives disappeared. She found it exciting that her Inner Self could come up with a solution to a decades-old problem just by being asked.

Sadness. A second major feeling we often hide is sadness. It comes in many forms: hurt, grief, despair, or anguish. Sadness often follows a loss, perhaps the loss of a love, self-esteem, or an important goal. It is often kept well hidden out of fear of embarrassment or because we have been trained that it is not noble to show our hurt.

Dirk used Bodymind Centering to get in touch with his difficulties in forming close relationships with women. As he explored this issue, he was drawn to what he described as a "dead zone" in his chest. As he worked with this sensation over several sessions he realized that he felt a bottomless well of old sadness in his chest. His dead zone was a way of keeping those feelings hidden. The sadness had to do with the despair of seeing his parents' battles as a child, and of not being able to make them be happy. He felt like he was the only child on the block whose parents were not happy.

As he repeatedly tuned in to the sadness, Dirk felt it release. Awareness flooded back into the dead zone, and he felt more alive. Not long after his experience, he met a woman through his work, and they began a satisfying relationship.

Fear. Fear is one of our most hidden emotions. How many of us are given permission to feel as scared as we felt as children? In many families fear is considered a sign of weakness to be covered at all cost. The truth seems to be that fear is absolutely normal, a part of everyday life. It occurs in all sorts of situations and is certainly not something to be ashamed of. But learning these simple truths can be time-consuming, unless you approach this issue directly, such as with Bodymind Centering.

A married couple used Bodymind Centering to solve problems and deepen their relationship. Barry and Cynthia often had the feeling of being "stuck" in their relationship. This feeling made their disputes hang on for longer than necessary. Even after they had intellectually resolved the dispute, they continued to have the "stuck" feelings. As they took each other through Bodymind Centering, they realized that they were both deeply afraid of change. Although their fear of change came from totally different traumas in their early lives, it was basically the same feeling they shared. Once they saw what the stuckness was really about, it disappeared from their relationship.

Fear is not a cathartic emotion, as are anger and sadness. In other words, sadness can be relieved through the catharsis of crying; fear cannot. Fear must be resolved through becoming aware of it. Bodymind Centering, since it is the application of awareness in a very specific way, can be very helpful in clearing up fears of various kinds.

Sexual feelings. Sex is still a subject of much confusion, even in the relatively free climate of today. We are only 100 years from the Victorian era when sex was hidden at all (and often high) costs. Today it is still hard for many parents to talk to their children about sexual feelings. Ideally children would learn that their sexual feelings are natural, and that they must express those feelings in ways that have only positive consequences for them. How many of us got these messages clearly from our parents? The authors have asked this question in workshops around the country and have found less than 10 percent of those surveyed received any sort of clear communication about sex from their parents.

You may find as you do Bodymind Centering that you have more sexual feelings than you realized. It is natural for human beings to have sexual feelings about many different people as they go through the day. You probably would not

71

want to express all those feelings, but it is important not to hide those feelings from yourself.

Dennis, a dentist in his mid-forties, was quite happily married, but suddenly found himself impotent with his wife. Using Bodymind Centering, he discovered that the impotence had begun when he had felt sexually attracted to his new dental assistant. He had shut off his sexual feelings toward her for fear of acting on them, and in so doing he had shut off his sexual feelings in general. When he fully acknowledged his sexual feelings and allowed himself to feel them, his sexual desire for his wife returned immediately.

Today, men and women are together much more than in the past. They are side by side in the workplace, often spending more hours there than with their own spouses or lovers. With this greater proximity, it is natural that more sexual feelings will arise. When people allow themselves to feel their sexual feelings, they are much less likely to act on them inappropriately. It sounds paradoxical, but actually seems to be true. Repression of sexual feelings is what causes their expression in troublesome ways.

Many human problems are caused by hiding true feelings, particularly sexual ones. Through Bodymind Centering, you may come to acknowledge your sexual feelings as a more integral part of yourself, and by so doing you may find greater freedom to be who you really are.

Happiness. You may find that you discover greater happiness inside than you knew was there as you practice Bodymind Centering. There are at least two reasons for this result. First, you may find that some of your inner joy has been covered over by other issues, problems or feelings. When you clear away the other issues your joy may emerge more clearly. Sometimes we get so busy trying to feel okay that we forget how magnificent we are deep inside. A second reason is that true happiness comes from having IS and OS aligned. When there is no gap between who you are inside and who you are outside, then you have earned the right to be truly happy. This is quite rare but entirely possible. Since Bodymind Centering is designed to work directly on unifying IS and OS, it can bring about more happiness than you have previously felt.

Guilt. When you explore your Inner Self with Bodymind Centering, you may come across things you have done that you wish you had not, and things you didn't do that you wish you had. This is guilt, and in the memorable words of one of the authors' clients, it feels "like you've been mosquito-bit all over."

Partway through a Bodymind Centering, May gasped, "I killed my mother." Now, May did not actually kill her mother. What had really happened was that she had asked her mother, age 88, to make a will during her final illness. It was necessary that she do so, and May's brothers and sisters elected May to ask her mother because she was the closest to her. Her mother died within an hour after signing the will. May felt guilty, even though intellectually she knew she did not cause her mother's death. After May realized how guilty she felt, her depression lifted.

Approval patterns. In Bodymind Centering, many people have uncovered issues of approval and disapproval. Many of us get entangled in seeking the approval of others. In the same way, some people live in constant fear of disapproval. These patterns start early for most people, usually because of overly critical parents.

Wendy, a teacher in her mid-twenties, worked on her tendency to be self-critical. As she tuned in to the pattern, she realized she could not remember a single incident of approval from her parents. Checking with her siblings, she found that they could not recall any either. It's no wonder that she had internalized the pattern and employed it as a major way of relating to herself.

Control patterns. With Bodymind Centering, you will often uncover issues of control. These are usually issues of over-control. For example, you may realize that you over-control your feelings to the extent that you don't let yourself feel much at all. Or you may discover that you put a lot of energy into trying to control people, or even whole situations. A great many problems come from people's attempts to over-control themselves and others.

A lawyer named Larry came for counseling because of his difficulty in making and sustaining friendships. Using Bodymind Centering to solve the issue, he came to a number of related insights: that he was rigid and controlling with himself (so that he let himself have very little fun), that he tried to control his friends (who eventually pulled away from him), and that his control problems came primarily from his relationship with his powerful father, also a lawyer. The issue of control pervaded his life. Much work on his part had to go into loosening his grip on himself and others.

Traumas. Through Bodymind Centering, you can work through old traumas in a safe and gentle way. Since you are always in charge of how far you want to go, there is no danger of being overwhelmed with material from your Inner Self.

Martina, a therapist in her thirties, had been physically and sexually abused by her father as a child. As an adult, her sexual relationships were often clouded by memories of the past traumas. By using Bodymind Centering every few days with a colleague from her office, Martina was able to separate out her present sexual relationships from the painful old memories. She began to have more satisfying relationships, and her perspective shifted in regard the past troubles with her father. She still does not have a good relationship with her father, and perhaps she never will, but at least she no longer lets the past intrude on the present.

Positive potentials. One of the most exciting discoveries that people make using Bodymind Centering is that within them are potentials of which they were

73

not aware. Not all of us have the potential to be Meryl Streep or Georgia O'Keeffe, but most of us have a great deal more potential than we are using. Here are several examples of potentials that people have uncovered with Bodymind Centering:

- a talent for drawing and painting, set aside years before due to family demands;
- a desire to return to college;
- the urge to ride and own a horse;
- the desire to have a private retreat place;
- a talent for singing, squelched 25 years before because of negative experiences with a singing teacher.

Within the Inner Self are many skills, powers and potentials that remain to be discovered. Many people have been surprised by the power of Bodymind Centering to help them learn how to be more of themselves.

The Basic Bodymind Centering Technique

If you are ready to begin, find a place where you can be quiet for 15-30 minutes. It is easiest if you have a friend take you through the steps. He or she can read the "script" while you fully relax into the experience. If you are doing Bodymind Centering by yourself, you will need a tape recorder to record the instructions, so that you can participate as you play it back to yourself. (Note: The Hendricks Institute has audio tapes of Bodymind Centering and other relaxation practices available. Please see page 125 for ordering information.) It is not useful to try to read Bodymind Centering and do it at the same time because reading takes you out of the relaxed state of mind that Bodymind Centering promotes.

If you have questions after you finish this section, turn to the next section. There, you will find answers to the most frequently asked questions about Bodymind Centering.

(The following instructions are to be read verbatim, except for the words in parentheses which are instructions to the person who is reading Basic Bodymind Centering.)

Find a place to sit reclining where your body is comfortably supported. You can have your eyes open or closed, although most people have eyes closed during this activity.

1. Let your attention turn toward your inner experience . . . (Pause here for ten seconds. Any time you see three dots, pause for ten seconds.) Notice the sounds you hear

outside the room . . . and in the room . . . Be aware of any sounds you hear inside . . . Notice where your body is contacting the chair and where that contact is harder or softer . . . Notice the kinds of thoughts moving through your mind right now . . . Be aware of any visual images or colors in your mind . . .

2. Be aware of the rise and fall of your breath . . . Let your in-breath roll easily over into your out-breath . . . Imagine your in-breath filling a pink balloon resting in your center that gently deflates as you breathe out (pause for 30 seconds).

3. Let your attention move slowly down your body . . . to your jaw and neck . . . your shoulders and chest . . . to your center . . . through your hips and thighs . . . your calves and ankles . . . through the soles of your feet . . .

4. Now focus your attention on some part of your body that feels tense . . . Simply keep noticing its shape . . . Notice its weight . . . Notice its size . . . Be aware of its texture . . . Notice any color (pause 30 seconds). Now turn your attention to another tense or tight area of your body and notice its size . . . Notice its shape . . . Notice how heavy or light it is . . . See if it has any color (pause 30 seconds).

5. Now let your mind sort through some current concerns that are important or troublesome to you. Just allow your mind to bring up any concerns (pause 20-30 seconds).

6. Bring your attention to one concern you'd like to explore today . . . Let your mind review that concern in detail . . . Allow your mind to give you images or thoughts about this concern . . . As this happens, allow yourself to keep focusing on your body sensations . . . Let your mind unwind in its way while you keep gently focusing on your body sensations (pause 20 seconds).

7. Now, listen to the following questions and let your body sensations, your Inner Self, answer . . .

What is my body experience of this issue? (Pause 15-20 seconds)

Have I felt this before? (Pause 15-20 seconds)

What is the core of this issue? (Let your Inner Self answer in whatever way.) (Pause 15-20 seconds)

Am I willing to have this issue clear up? (Pause 15-20 seconds)

Is this issue about controlling or being controlled? (Pause 15-20 seconds)

Am I trying to look good? (Pause 15-20 seconds)

What do I need to learn here? (Pause 15-20 seconds)

What feelings are incomplete? (Pause 15-20 seconds)

Is there anything I need to do or say? To whom? (Pause 15-20 seconds)

What about this concern needs to be loved? (Pause 15-20 seconds)

8. Now notice a place inside that seems connected to this concern . . . Look at it . . . Hear, feel and taste it . . . Gently bring your attention to that place again and again until you experience a shift in that place in your body . . . Nod when you sense a shift . . . (Pause until your partner nods, or give yourself 30-40 seconds' pause if you are recording a tape for yourself.) Notice another place that seems connected to this concern . . . Look at it . . . Hear, feel and taste it . . . Gently bring your attention to that place again and again until you experience a shift in that place in your body . . . Note when you sense a shift . . .

9. Now take a few minutes to fluff the issue and your body with your breath. Be aware of any place that needs fluffing and gently breathe into and around it (pause 30-60 seconds).

10. Let yourself love the concern and your experience for a moment or two before easily stretching and opening your eyes.

11. Take a few moments to note down any discoveries. Remember that insights often come later when you're moving on through life.

Frequently Asked Questions About Bodymind Centering

*A*s we have done Bodymind Centering with people over the years, we have collected questions they have asked after first trying the technique. In this section we will give answers to some of the most frequently-asked questions.

What if I do Bodymind Centering and nothing happens?
Few people have dramatic, "aha!" experiences the first time they do Bodymind Centering. In fact, we recommend that you judge the effects of Bodymind Centering by its results in your life, rather than by the nature of the experiences you have while you are actually doing it. This is because it is a subtle process, and the power of it does not always register on you while you are doing it.

What is the Inner Self?
The Inner Self is the part of us that knows how we really feel. The Inner Self is intu-

itive, gets hunches, and comprehends whole situations, but it does not focus on specifics. As we grow up we often have to hide the Inner Self in order to survive. With time, we often lose touch with it entirely, so that it has to speak to us through pains, tension, dreams, accidents and other roundabout ways. Through Bodymind Centering, Inner Self and Outer Self are reconnected.

What is resistance?

Resistance is anything you do to avoid going deeper into yourself. It is natural because most of us are afraid of really being who we are. While you are doing Bodymind Centering, you may encounter resistance in many forms. You may suddenly get bored or sleepy, or you may remember that you have something else you "just have to do." Whatever form your resistance takes, simply stay with it, notice it, explore it, and find out what's at the bottom of it.

What is a shift?

For most people, it is a physical sensation of something changing. It can also be a thought or an image. It is a "just-noticeable" difference, be it tiny or huge.

Why do shifts occur?

Consciousness has healing power, so when you focus consciousness on yourself you activate a healing process. If you allow it, consciousness will move its healing presence from one place to another that needs it.

After Bodymind Centering, I can't remember what happened. Should I take notes?

If you wish, take a few notes right afterwards. It may not be necessary, though, to remember what happened. The Inner Self has no sense of self-consciousness, so changes frequently happen without knowing why or how. Also, when a problem clears up, it simply disappears from your memory.

Does Bodymind Centering result in big emotional releases?

Often not. Bodymind Centering addresses a deeper level than that in which feelings occur, so big catharses are not typical. It is fine if they occur, particularly if the person has been holding on to something for a long time, but you probably won't see as many emotional releases as with other forms of therapy.

What should I do to make Bodymind Centering work if the person I am doing it with is not willing?

Don't do Bodymind Centering with anyone who does not really want to do it. This process is for willing people.

Is it okay to lie down instead of sitting up during Bodymind Centering?
We usually recommend the sitting position, since lying down often makes people fall asleep.

Moving Centered

*T*he following variation of Bodymind Centering is designed to involve you in connecting kinesthetically with the Inner Self and solving problems. It helps you "get out of your head" and acknowledge the resources and information of your moving body. As we suggested with Bodymind Centering, you will have the best experience if you have someone read the instructions or if you tape them to follow.

Find a comfortable lying down position and close your eyes. Take a few moments to gently stretch, wiggle, and shift your body in whatever ways will allow you to be more comfortable.

1. Notice whatever is passing through your mind: thoughts, images, sounds. (Pause ten seconds)

2. Let your awareness move gently through your body, noticing any areas that call your attention. (Pause ten seconds, then repeat steps 1 and 2 two more times)

3. Again notice whatever is arising in your mind . . . and be aware of your hands. Go back and forth between noticing thoughts and images and noticing your hands until you feel a bridge or link between them. (Pause twenty to thirty seconds)

4. Notice the speed of what arises in your mind, and allow your hands to move to match that pace, fast or slow, jerky or smooth. (Pause thirty seconds)

5. Return to your mind again and notice other qualities of what passes by: scattered, buzzing, plodding, empty, repetitious, soaring (pause ten seconds). Let your hands move to match the qualities you notice in your mind. Let your awareness focus on just how it is, releasing should's and the need to do it right. As you move, qualities may shift . . . follow any shifts with your hands. (Pause thirty seconds)

6. Now scan your body with your awareness. Notice where your body feels hard against the floor . . . and where there is space. Notice where you feel most alive . . . and where your breath moves in you. (Pause twenty to thirty seconds)

7. Notice the part of your body that next emerges in your awareness and let your hands move to match the way that part feels. Allow more involvement of your body as you move. (Pause twenty to thirty seconds)

8. Now notice a tense part of your body. Let your hands describe its shape and weight and texture as they lead the rest of your body in movement. Then pause and rest. (Pause twenty to thirty seconds)

9. Let another body part come to your attention, and allow your breath to fill it. (Pause twenty seconds)

10. Now let a problem or issue come into your mind, and notice how your body feels as you think of the issue. (Pause ten to twenty seconds)

11. Let your hands and body move with the WHOLE-BODY FEELING of that issue until a shift occurs, then pause and rest. (Pause until hands are resting again)

12. Let another problem or issue come into your mind, and notice your WHOLE-BODY FEELING as you think of it. (Pause ten to twenty seconds)

13. Allow your hands and body to move with the WHOLE-BODY FEELING of the issue until you feel a shift, then pause and rest. (Pause until hands are resting again)

14. Spend a few moments appreciating yourself and loving your body, then gently return your awareness to the outside.

(Discuss as long as client wishes.)

CHAPTER SEVEN

On Getting What You Want: Our Method of Manifestation

For some years now we have been offering training in the principles and practices of manifestation. The body of knowledge presented in these trainings has come largely from information revealed during meditation. Other parts of the material have appeared in response to questions or comments during the trainings. These two sources have yielded a substantial oral tradition which has been lovingly collected by students, and passed along through notes and anecdotes. Now, since large numbers of people want to experiment with these materials, we have set out to make this oral tradition available in an intact, concise form for the private student or the teacher of manifestation.

In writing this chapter, we have tried to present the material in the most brief and trimmed-down form possible. Our conviction is that even the most potent and evolved ideas should be be presented simply and clearly. The ideas are here to be used as tools for experimentation, rather than to enhance anyone's belief system. The scientific method—try it and observe the results—is the best model we have found to guide us in the realm of manifestation.

How Unconscious Manifestation Works

Long before you consider manifesting what you consciously want, you have had years of experience with unconscious manifestion. Conscious manifestation begins to work more smoothly once you see what you have been doing in the past. The best way to find out what unconscious manifestation you have been producing in your life is simply to observe the results you have created. The negative results you create *are* your unconscious.

This point cannot be overemphasized. You need to see that the way it is now is the way you have chosen it to be on some level. Knowing this, you are in a better position to move smoothly on to creating more positive consciousness. Unfortunately, many people keep pretending that they are helpless bystanders in a life that's doing it to them. This point of view puts personal evolution on hold until they acknowledge that they are the source of what they manifest.

Roles

*B*y adopting the conditions of a particular role, you will tend to manifest those aspects which are associated with that role. If you are programmed toward a role as a doctor, for example, you will tend to manifest more money than if you are conditioned to the role of gardener. Much of the manifestation we unconsciously create begins simply by stepping into a role which is circumscribed by traditional agreements and expectations. There are general mores that govern various roles in life, and by stepping into a certain role you assume the mores to your benefit or detriment. Doctors make ten times as much money as clerks; they also commit suicide seven times as often. So, extraordinary skill is not a necessary condition for most doctors to make money, but skill may be required to remain healthy and happy.

On the down side, roles can create havoc in manifestation.

Forgetting that we have assumed unconscious contracts by claiming a specific role, we can confound our conscious desires. The doctor who does not explore why doctors commit suicide at seven times the normal rate is setting up problems for him- or herself. There are certain compelling psychological issues that trouble doctors that do not trouble clerks.

Another troublesome issue is not freely selecting our roles. We have worked with many prosperous and effective people who have excelled in a role only to find misery in their achievement. When they inquire about the origin for such a seeming contradiction, they often find a compromise at the source, where they have overridden their deepest desires. For example, we recently worked with a very successful developer who really wanted to be a sculptor. Not much money in art, his parents constantly admonished. After several lucrative but lonely years living in the developer role, he has now consciously rearranged his life to make time for his passion. Ironically, the creativity released by sculpting has also increased his business productivity.

We often repeat roles exactly the way we observed them in early life. For example, we may reenact the role of a martyr parent because our own parents sacrificed and suffered. It may not even occur to us that it is possible to have fun being a parent.

Roles also function as cultural transmitters, particularly of traditional masculine and feminine behavior. For example, women are expected to take primary responsibility for home and family, no matter what other work they may do. Men are expected to produce no matter how they feel. We learn and incorporate thousands of nonverbal gender messages before we enter school. Most adults still function through these unconscious filters that color every manifestation.

AN EXPERIMENT

Note: Each major section of this chapter closes with an experiment designed to make practical the teaching in the section. In the practices, the procedure is as follows:

1. Sit comfortably, eyes closed if you wish.

2. Rest for 30-60 seconds.

3. Begin the experiment. In the experiment that follows, ask each question silently, then pause for 10-15 seconds to allow space for your mind and body to respond. The information may come in an unusual form. You may ask a question, for example, and the answer may come in the form of an energy fluctuation in your body.

4. When you finish the experiment, rest for a minute or so before returning to normal awareness.

QUESTIONS FOR MEDITATION

- What roles have I taken on in my life?
- To what extent are my roles freely chosen?
- How much of what I manifest (positive and negative) is due to my roles?

Incompletions

*M*uch of what we unconsciously manifest is due to nature's abhorrence of incompletion. Humans leave many things incomplete in the face of a strong drive in nature toward completion. By holding fast to a pattern of incompletion, and overriding nature's strong pull toward completion, we are propelled into one confusing situation after another.

There are several key areas in which we tend to have incompletions. One is in the area of feelings we do not let ourselves feel. A monk may separate himself from his sexuality in order to form his "good monk" ego, only to find later that he keeps returning to the subject of sex in his attempts to meditate. We are drawn toward wholeness, and nature will keep presenting to us anything that we leave incomplete. It seems that anything we shun will come back to us later to be embraced. If we hold tightly to our personalities in the face of repeated opportunitites to embrace wholeness, we lock ourselves into cycles of conflict with ourselves.

In my own life (GH), I was heavily conditioned toward a nice-guy persona. That is the way my saintly father was; and although he died shortly after I was conceived, somehow I knew that I had to be that way, too. I sealed off the emotion of anger because it was inconsistent with my nice-guy facade. For thirty years I never showed anger. People around me were always getting angry, often at me, but I simply regarded them as illogical fools.

Then I had a profound realization. I actually was angry, though it was buried deep inside, and because I was cut off from it, I required people around me to act it out for me. Buried it was; I weighed over a hundred pounds more than I do now. So I went about the task of reowning all that old anger and training myself to be able to communicate it instead of keeping it inside. I did not find the task to be an easy one, nor do I now. Even after fifteen years of working with the issue, I still notice that I am faced with an almost daily choice of disowning anger or claiming and using the energy from it.

Nature has evolved a strategy for dealing with incompletions that is very benign, although it may strike us as maddening until we learn to use it to our benefit. If an incompletion occurs, nature provides us with subsequent opportunities to complete it. For example, if you need to complete a communication with your father, you may find yourself in repeated situations with your father or people who resemble him. Some incompletions may seem trivial by themselves until we look for a theme. For example, a man expressed a desire to have a better relationship with money and to have more abundance. When we inquired into incompletions around money, it turned out he owed many people small sums of money. The combined effect of these debts was like a swarm of bees irritating and sapping his exchange of money with the world. As he consolidated his debts and took responsibility for completing them he began to see opportunities to create more abundance on many levels, including more money. Each situation has within it the opportunity to deliver the communication and dissolve the pattern.

An incompletion may also occur with regard to a positive potential that has not been acknowledged. For example, a woman may not have acknowledged and expressed a strong-man archetype that lies dormant within her. She may keep running into and competing with strong men outside herself—father, husband, policeman, judge—until she owns her inner strong man. When she accepts and expresses this positive energy, she may find that she manifests a different relationship with the strong men in her outer world.

QUESTIONS FOR MEDITATION

- What feelings do I not like to feel?
- What unfinished business do I have left over from past relationships?
- What do I still need to say to people in my past?
- What do I need to do to complete my unfinished relationships?
- What positive energies do I need to open up to?

Manifestation through Conscious Thought

A person can manifest what he/she wants by consciously using the powers of the mind to design its own reality. People are geniuses at manifestation; often, though, that genius is harnessed to the unconscious. In therapy over the years, we have had many opportunities to marvel at people's talent for manifestation. A person may, after years of abuse, finally divorce an alcoholic spouse only to find and marry another alcoholic within a short time. What are the odds of such an occurrence?

It is clear to anyone reading this book that we create our own reality. As we saw in the first section, this reality is often created unconsciously by fulfilling roles, by resisting feelings, or by holding back on positive energies that could be expressed.

One barrier to conscious manifestation is the fear of figuring out what we really want. We worry that we will manifest something and it will turn out to be detrimental to our overall evolution. In using conscious thought, we simply have to go by trial and error, doing our best at figuring out what we want, manifesting it, and then making corrections if it is not quite right. There is friction in the Newtonian world (the world of conscious thought), so manifestation is likely to be not quite right. Indeed, we learn as much from the misses as the hits. In other words, it is all right to mess up and correct. People sometimes express a fear that their manifestation will mess up in a big way, like King Midas, or that a huge black hole will open in the universe and swallow their best intentions. To address this issue we suggest The Cosmic Clause to end any manifestation experiment: "May all my manifestations have totally beneficial consequences for me, others, and the universe."

How Do I Know What to Want

*I*n our manifestation workshops we spend considerable time on figuring out what people really want. We usually begin by having people brainstorm their five end-goals. Personally speaking, we have done this exercise many times, always with value. You ask yourself the five goals that would make your life a success. Imagine that you are on your deathbed and someone asks "Was your life a success?" You say,

"Yes, because I accomplished these five things . . . " Or you reply that your life was a failure because you did not accomplish the five things. What are those five things for you right now? Of course they may change over time, but what are they this moment?

In figuring out what you want, be willing to be creative. In other words, just dream it up. Many people think that there are a stack of sacred wants lying dormant down in their cells, and that these will flow up into consciousness with the proper access. Perhaps this is true, but in the meantime, ask yourself: What do I want? Accept the trivial and the profound. Your mind and body are usually not used to asking this question, and therefore it may take some practice, but with time you will likely be able to come up with something that you know for sure that you want.

Another hint: Put your wants in a positive framework. Instead of "I want people to stay off my back," want something positive, such as "I want complete freedom and autonomy." Just wanting people off your back results from anger instead of a desire to create something new and original in your life.

Now, let's find out how we can connect our natural powers of mind with conscious thought. This can be done in several ways. Mental pictures, language and feelings can be used to describe the reality we wish to create. We have found that some people have more power through using mental pictures. Others find that feeling works best for them, while still others find they are more successful with language. Experiment with all three to find out which one, or which combination, works best.

TO USE MENTAL PICTURES

1. Sit comfortably with eyes closed.

2. Pick an area of manifestion:
   a. Material things—car, house, money, job.
   b. Relationships—clear up a problem, create a new person in your life, etc.
   c. Life purpose—right now or in general.
   d. Psychological/spiritual.

3. Picture what you want. Let a number of pictures come until you get a good feel for one or more.

4. View it from top, bottom and sides.

5. Continue with another area of manifestation or return to normal awareness.

TO USE FEELING

1. Pick an area.

2. Sit comfortably. Close your eyes if you wish.

3. Feel what you want. Use your body to feel it intensely. Notice if your body wants to move in any way as you focus on what you want. Follow any impulses to move, however large or small.

4. Feel it to completion, i.e., until it dissolves and your attention moves on.

5. Go to another area of manifestation or return to normal awareness.

TO USE LANGUAGE

1. Pick an area.

2. Sit comfortably. Close your eyes if you wish.

3. Say a sentence in your mind that embodies what you want to manifest. Use "I am willing" as the opening of each sentence. We use this phrase because willingness means you are open to it but not attached.

    Examples: "I am willing to have the perfect new car manifest in my life" or "I am willing to have an improved relationship with my boss."

4. Say the sentence, then let it go and let your mind rest for ten to fifteen seconds. Repeat; rest. Do this several times until you feel it settle into place.

5. Now feel how it would be to have whatever you are working on.
    Say in your mind in the present tense "I have a perfect new car" or "I have a good relationship with my boss." Translate everything into the present tense. Say the sentence, then rest for ten to fifteen seconds, then repeat. Continue until you can actually believe that you have it.

6. After a minute or two with one project, go one to another or return to normal awareness.

With all forms of manifestion, your willingness and sincerity give them power. Only those things which you put "heart" behind tend to manifest. When checking the results of your experiences, the image of space and fog may be useful. If you bounce the beam of your manifestation directly off space, or that which has "heart," you are much more likely to create what you want. If you don't get quite what you want, you are beaming off the fog of incompletions.

HOW TO CLEAR UP THE FOG

1. Clear up any unfelt feelings about the situation. Feelings are cleared the moment you become willing to feel them.

2. Give attention to any body trauma associated with the situation after the mind is willing (do breathwork, get a massage, have acupressure, etc.).

3. Clear up any mixed motives (any unconscious motive dragged along with the clear motive, such as needing approval or to be right). When you broadcast two motives, the unconscious one will manifest.

Hits and Misses

Newtonian manifestation most effectively deals with in-the-world projects. Corrections and adjustment are the operative modes as you work in this realm. We have several examples of how people have used Newtonian manifestation. Cars, houses and jobs come up most frequently, although one woman who was very oriented toward agendas and lists used conscious thought manifestation to create a long list of the qualities she wanted in a mate. She missed her next appointment because she had already met this man and was moving east to marry him.

One man manifested a new sports car and shortly thereafter got caught in a hail storm that destroyed the finish of the car. He inquired into any unconscious motivation that he might have brought to the situation and discovered an old belief that he couldn't be too flashy or have anything too flashy. A woman was rear-ended in new cars three times before she realized that she needed to complete an old "pain in the neck" relationship. Another woman drove a classic, beat-up old VW for ten years that regularly broke down and never went very fast, but it was familiar and comfortable. When she cleared up her scarcity attitude and her fears of becoming scattered and ungrounded if she went too fast in her life, she manifested a gorgeous, powerful car quite easily.

Several years ago we wanted to move into a house where we could work as well as live. I (KH) worked with Newtonian manifestation to picture and feel the perfect space. A friend called a few days later to let us know that a house near him was available and hadn't gone on the market yet. We went to look at it, and I saw that I had left a few things out of the order. The living room/work space was just as I had imagined with a large open space, plently of light, wood floors, and a fireplace. However, the kitchen was very old and tiny, there was no bathroom upstairs, and the whole space was too small for our family. So I went back to the drawing board. About a week later our friend called and said the new owners were remodeling the house, completely redoing the kitchen and putting in a bathroom upstairs. We moved in within the month and enjoyed the house for several years.

A talented woman recently used Newtonian manifestation to create a new job. Twice in the previous year she had been a finalist for good jobs and had lost to an "insider." She was again a finalist for her perfect job and again competing with an insider. She realized she was afraid to go all out and lose again. We worked to clear up old feelings of not being good enough and holding back, and she used all the Newtonian principles to imagine herself in this position. She called excitedly soon after to say she got the job.

Intentions

*I*n manifestation, we are learning to use the mind as an active force rather than a reactive one. In growing up, most of us learn to think of ourselves as simply reacting to what is going on around us; others call the shots, and we follow along. Later in life we have to correct this distortion if we really want to use our full power.

Our intentions, or basic motivations, are the most powerful forces that operate to shape our actions. If our basic motivations are reactive, they do not serve us the way we are now. For example, to survive in your particular family as a child, you may have developed a basic motivation of seeking approval. All your actions may have been actually reactions; one eye was always on getting approval. You have, then, two basic motivations or intentions: Survival + Approval. Suppose that you were also occasionally punished for doing things you thought you would get approval for. You may have collected a lot of anger about this unpredictability. You did not know how to express this anger so you had to control it. Your basic motivations become: Survival + Approval + Control. Note that all these are reactive; you choose them as a way of dealing with a difficult situation. They are not the result of going deeply into yourself and figuring out what you really want.

Here are two radically transformative things you can do to change basic motivations. One is to choose consciously an entirely new motivation and allow it to settle into your mind. A new motivation might be something like: My intention now is for all my actions to serve the highest creative force in my life and in the universe. A motivation like this goes beyond the old, reactive motivations because it is much more comprehensive. In addition, it is freely chosen by you.

A second approach is to choose a motivation that directly counters one of the old ones. For example, if you wish to replace your approval-seeking motivation, you can choose an intention like: I am now willing to provide my own approval.

Both these approaches bring about a very rapid shift in consciousness and in the results we get in life. They also flush up a lot of debris, the flotsam and jetsam of old structures, that will need to be cleaned up through bodywork, completing communications, etc.

Manifestation through Einsteinian Principles

*T*here is a quicker and more powerful method of manifestation than using conscious thought. It makes use of the principles of physics described by Albert Einstein. Here is not the place to go into the technical aspects of the physics, but for the sake of having an intellectual foundation for the experiments we will carry out, let us say that Einstein came up with a very wild idea. He observed that the nature of reality changes with the speed of the observer. In plain psychological terms, if we are vibrating at a very low speed, we will see and experience things differently than if we are vibrating at a higher rate. What determines our speed of vibration? Awareness and love. This principle has been responsible for thousands of miracles in our lives and in the lives of people with whom we have had the pleasure of working over the years.

A further expression of this idea is that we not only experience reality differently as we vibrate at higher rates, but our presence in the situation changes the vibration level of the whole situation. We see it differently, and it becomes different as we see it. We would never ask anyone to believe such an outrageous idea; you simply will have to try it out for yourself and see how quickly things change.

Here are several examples of how awareness and love can bring about sudden, positive change. I (GH) was once feeling deeply afraid, and didn't see any way out. Then I remembered awareness and love. I opened up to the fear, felt it fully in my body, and then loved it the way it was. It changed instantly. I was no longer afraid; I was in ecstasy. The fear never returned.

A man was feeling stuck in an unpleasant relationship with his ex-wife. His position was that her anger was causing all the problems. Then one day he stopped projecting, opened up to his own anger, and loved it. Instantly, he found himself able to love her anger, too. Immediately after this experience their whole relationship went through a shift and ceased to be a problem.

A young woman who had struggled with alcohol and drug abuse, suicidal episodes and many physical ailments began to realize that she was paralyzed by fear almost all the time. She didn't breathe fully, her body was held rigidly, her face was like a mask, and she felt lonely and isolated much of the time. When she actively loved her fear, experienced it and participated fully with it, it began to melt. She noticed the exquisite colors and smells in nature. Supportive friends started to call and spend time with her. She got an acknowledgement for the first time at work. She began to enjoy being alive.

The principles work for all types of manifestation. If you want a new job, for example, love yourself for not liking the one you have. Love it the way it is, and it starts to change. The more thoroughly and fully it is loved, the more rapid and positive the transformation.

This technique seems too simple to be so powerful. Many people do not get around to trying it until all else has failed.

The only drawback to this technique is that it works so fast that it seems unpredictable. People often try it, experience a radical change, then get scared because they did not realize they had so much power.

For example, on a Thursday night several years ago I (KH) felt a clear resolve to claim my full power and to open up to initiating and creating my life consciously. Gay and I talked about what that might mean, how it might look, to the point that I had a vivid body sense of willingness to open to power. Then we went on with the evening, dancing and enjoying being together.

At about two in the morning I woke up knowing I was going to be sick. I made my way quietly to the bathroom and vomited, then came back to bed. After about twenty minutes the cycle repeated, and soon I had diarrhea also. Throughout the early morning hours I was up and down, trying not to bother Gay. At one point Gay said, "How are you doing?" I had completely forgotten about the evening's intention and discussion. By six o'clock I was downstairs on the floor in the bathroom, having tried everything I knew to stop the cycle, which was moving into convulsions by then.

Gay came in then and asked if I wanted some assistance. I said, "Yes, please," and he sat on my pelvis. I realized I had been trying not to feel my pelvis and to get out of it by writhing and rolling. When the weight of Gay's body brought my awareness fully to my pelvis, I instantly experienced a white-hot fury. The collective anger of generations of oppressed women rolled through me. On its heels came the fear of what "they" would do to me if I was fully powerful. I was terrified I would be killed if I let people really see my power. These feelings consumed my body for about ten minutes, and then I was entirely peaceful. I felt tired, but whole. Over the next days I traced the pattern of previous vomiting episodes in my life and integrated the common thread of anger and fear. One effect of that intention was that competition with women was replaced by the free flow of support. The intention to empower each other makes being with women a joy and a creative force in our worlds.

Here are two experiments to give you a feel for how it works. The first experiment uses Einsteinian principles to eliminate something from your life; the second experiment creates something new or something more in your life.

EXPERIMENT #1

1. Sit comfortably.

2. Pick something you want to clear up or make disappear. (Examples: a feeling like fear, anger or sadness; a problem relationship; a situation that seems intractable.)

3. Love it the way it is.

4. Find where you feel it in your body. Love that place.

5. Love it until you feel a shift.

6. Pick something else or return to normal awareness.

EXPERIMENT #2

1. Sit comfortably.

2. Pick something you want, or something you want more of (e.g., money, a new relationship, a new job).

3. Love yourself for wanting it.

4. Love it the way it is now.

5. Find it in your body; love it there.

6. Keep loving it until you feel a shift.

7. Pick something else or return to normal awareness.

Positions

We have often heard people say with great frustration, "I thought I had gotten rid of THAT!" The belief that at some point we arrive and cease evolving is an example of taking a position. Positions freeze our unfolding until we become aware of their stuck quality and the flatness of our experience. Even "good" positions such as "I'm going to love everyone no matter what!" can limit our possible transformation. Positions often take the form of attachment to attitudes and beliefs, and are reflected in movement patterns and postures. Recognizing and releasing positions is a skill that increases flexibility and accelerates evolution. We have observed that beliefs have no evolutionary power; letting go of beliefs does.

This experiment is kinesthetically based, and is designed to be done with a partner. One person will facilitate the other moving through the entire sequence before switching.

1. Together, brainstorm the phrases, thoughts and beliefs that recur in your awareness. Some examples of core beliefs are:
    * I'm unlovable (not good enough);
    * I just can't do it;
    * I have to struggle to get anywhere;
    * If I do it well enough, I can go back to sleep;
    * You can't trust anyone;
    * Everything about me is wrong;
    * I won't.

2. Explore incorporating several of those attitudes or beliefs; let your body freeze in the metaphorical position of each belief. Facilitator: Assist and take on the mover's position in your own body. Exaggerate. Spend some time noticing tensions, breath, the familiarity of the posture.

3. Explore each of the following interventions with one of the positions. After each intervention, come back to the original held position before continuing.
    a. Facilitator, try to persuade the mover to let go of the position. Use primarily nonverbal techniques.
    b. Facilitator, try making the mover let go of the position (explore your method of using force).
    c. Both of you take on the mover's position and let your awareness move to the core of the position as you experience it in your bodies. Breathe into that place until energy starts to move. Let that place move your whole body from the inside out, following the shifts until each of you feels complete.
    d. Both of you be with the position and love it fully for what it was trying to do. Love all the fallout that emerges. Both of you move all the way with the energy.
    Take a few minutes to discuss your experience, then switch.

CHARACTERISTICS OF THE EINSTEINIAN WAY

1. Old rules (i.e., roles, beliefs, automatic reactions) dissolve and are no longer applicable.

2. Concern shifts to the rate of vibration. You come to see that your vibration level draws to you the appropriate action or lesson. You see that you are getting exactly what you are putting out.

3. Willingness becomes important, especially the willingness to:
- drop limiting beliefs at the moment they seem not to work;
- feel all your feelings, particularly the fear of death (lowest vibration) and the fear of going crazy (highest vibration);
- learn to occupy all parts of your body;
- release old, unmet needs;
- tell the deepest level of truth;
- keep your agreements;
- give and receive love completely (for example, in a stuck place, ask "What do I need to love more in order to be free of this game?");
- take total responsibility: acknowledge the way it is, and take responsibility NOW, without reference to the past.

The Third Way

*T*here is a third way of manifestation that we like to call, oddly enough, The Third Way. It is the most powerful form that we have yet found.

In Third Way manifestation, you align yourself with the source of energy and consciousness in the universe, the Big River, so that the energy propels and guides you, putting you in the right place at the right time for your desires to be immediately manifested. Nothing satisfies like the Big River flowing in complete relationship with all the potentials in you. People are drawn to the Big River with its currents of being, giving and allowing.

In The Third Way several things are required. You must be totally committed to serving the creative force of the universe. You must be open to the deepest energies within you. You must be willing to drop projection and excess ego baggage. You must be working on your mind and body constantly so that you can see, feel and follow currents of energy through the universe. You must tell the truth and keep your agreements.

As a bird soars higher, it must be more sensitive to the currents of air so the flight can be effortless even as the air gets thinner. So it is with Third Way manifestation. The requirements mentioned above are steep ones. They could be no less, because the powerful energies involved in Third Way manifestation require impeccability of action and a healthy, grounded nervous system. Otherwise we would be buffeted about to the detriment of our evolution.

Stepping into Third Way manifestation is a matter of free choice. You make the decision. Third Way energies are strong and will flush out anything in their way. That is why your free choice is required. No one but you will have to confront the material that is flushed out of you as you integrate Third Way energies. For example, if there is some feeling you have repressed, even long ago, it will likely be brought to the surface as you open up to Third Way energy.

Recently in the process of going more deeply into The Third Way, a memory came up of a $500 debt I (GH) had incurred over a decade ago. I had completely forgotten about it, perhaps because I had gotten into a conflict with the person not long after I borrowed the money. I had to write letters to find him, so I could initiate the process of paying off the debt. He was very surprised, and I felt a new lightness and energy in myself as a result. I noticed that the following year my income took a quantum jump. Of course, there is no way to prove that there was a causal relationship between the two events, but these same types of things have happened so many times that I have come to rely on them.

The deeper and higher we go with The Third Way, the more energy moves through us. We have to tell the truth to ourselves and others, and we have to honor our agreements to ourselves and others. This allows Third Way energies to stream through us freely. For example, if I create a new pattern in the universe (e.g., I agree to show up at the corner of Main and First Street at noon), I have to honor that pattern scrupulously. If I do not make good on the pattern I have created, a deep part of myself records this information and will prevent me from integrating more Third Way energy until I can have integrity enough to handle it.

People who are involved with this type of manifestation become very concerned with taking care of their minds and bodies. They tend to meditate regularly, eat high-vibration food, and polish their bodies through exercise and bodywork. After committing themselves to The Third Way, they know that various mental and physical blocks have to be dissolved. Many people find it easier to go after the blocks on a regular basis, rather than having the blocks come after them.

A major illusion that needs to be dissolved in order to integrate The Third Way is the separation between ourselves and the universe, ourselves and God. To live in The Third Way is to come from the source, to see and feel that we are God and the universe. It inhabits us; we are it, moving it from place to place.

The Third Way may take us a lifetime to integrate fully. No matter. It is our intention to live in The Third Way that carries us forward, opening the gate to the many miracles that this form of manifestation has in store for us.

To begin, here is an experiment:

1. Sit comfortably, eyes closed if you prefer.

2. In your mind, ask yourself the following questions. Phrase each question, then allow 10-15 seconds for your body and mind to process it. Don't worry if an "answer" fails to appear; it is the asking that is important. An answer may appear later in a

dream, or in an awareness long after you have forgotten about the question.

- Am I totally committed to serving the creative force in the universe?
- Am I willing to experience and express my deepest energies?
- Am I willing to live without projection and unnecessary personality?
- Am I committed to refining my mind and body?
- Am I willing to tell the truth?
- Am I willing to keep my agreements?
- Am I willing to dissolve my sense of separation between me and the universe?

3. After you finish, relax for a minute or two, then return to normal awareness.

CHARACTERISTICS OF THE THIRD WAY

1. Lax times when you have a minimum of stimulation or demands on your time (important for grounding and integrating the charge passing through).

2. Large vibrations passing through the body (signifying a deeper surrender to the universe).

3. The feeling that you have little or no choice, that you are guided, that you have "choiceless awareness."

4. Periods of inarticulateness or "mush mind." When awareness is spreading down the front of the body, moving from one zone to another, it crosses the transition point where one radiance zone passes into another (e.g., shifting from throat zone to heart). This transition creates mush mind. The time it takes to pass through mush mind is precisely how long it takes you to remember to move and breathe.

5. High-quality daily experience, with a bigger oscillation of intensity. Also, high-quality friends.

Using the Three Forms Together

*T*he three forms are extensions of each other and may be used in conjunction with one another. For example, you may start by using conscious thought to manifest a new car. You picture it, feel it, write a few willingness statements about it. Perhaps a few weeks go by and nothing happens. Either go back and refine your conscious thoughts, or drop into an Einsteinian mode by loving it the way it is. At this point you may "accidentally" come across someone at a party who wants to sell a car. In this example, you opened the gate with conscious thought, walked through with

*Even Simpler Instructions
for Conscious, Creative Manifestation*

1. *Take a deep breath, and pass through the gate of fear.
Everytime you manifest something successfully and go to a
higher level, you tend to pass through the gate of fear again.*

2. *Consciously conceive of it the way you want it.
Think up the kind of job, relationship, life you want.*

3. *Observe what you're getting at any moment,
love the way you feel about manifesting it,
then love the thing itself as much as you can.*

4. *Surrender yourself to your grandest, ultimate purpose
in relationship, work & life.
COSMIC HINT: It's usually what you most love to do,
the way you most love to feel,
what you most love to be.
Surrendering just means you do it more and more often.*

Einsteinian principles, then found yourself in the right place at the right time to manifest the original desire.

Generally, conscious thought works best with manifestations in the material world, while Einsteinian principles work best in the psychological and relationship domain. The Third Way is always useful because when you are in harmony with yourself and the universe, where and when you need to be, you always have what you want and need.

It can facilitate your journey to figure out what you really want in life. Being clear about what you want is important, as is setting the wheels in motion toward your goal, even if you are not sure how to get there. In fact, the most meaningful goals are those which you have absolutely no idea how to attain. I (GH) decided in 1979 that I wanted to take the spring of 1980 off, spending it traveling in India, Nepal and Europe. I set April 1, 1980 as my departure date. As the time approached, I found myself with a most excellent plan and very little money. My daughter had needed a number of things that year, and I had spent most of my savings on them. I recall describing the problem to a friend over breakfast a couple of months before I was to go. She immediately offered to loan me the money. I thanked her, but told her I was sure the money would appear from somewhere. Incredibly, I got a call one day from my mother in Florida. She was asking my permission to sell an acre of land that my father had bought in 1937. Neither my mother nor I previously had any idea the property was owned jointly by her, my brother and myself. To make a long story short, I got a check for $2,500 during March, allowing me to leave on schedule.

We think it is important to get the energy vectors aligned, even though you don't know how the physical aspects are going to emerge. Obviously, if you knew how to attain the goal, you would already be there. What is important, though, is to be clear on what you want, then start your energy moving in that direction.

What–Do–I–Want Experiment

*T*he experiential process of discovering and acting consciously on what we want is unique for each person. We make decisions when presented with external choices, and we generate choices from internal experience. We often have more practice with making choices than the environment seems to offer, and we make those choices using different internal maps. For example, when considering whether to go to a movie, one person may look at an internal image of the movie, then listen to an internal body sensation around the umbilicus which is a yes signal. Another person may hear the title of the movie and choose according to whether the sound is pleasant or unpleasant.

Responding to the question "What do you want in your life?" is unfamiliar to people. Parenting guides discussing choices for children often added the instruction to not leave things open-ended, but to say for example, "Do you want eggs or cereal this morning?" Asking "What do you want for breakfast?" was considered too chaotic for young children. The child might reply, "Ice cream with broccoli on top." Most of us haven't had much practice in inner-generated choosing. We think we have to choose from what is on the menu, rather than creating the menu. The following experiment is designed to help you discover your process for both internally and externally generated choice-making.

1. Get comfortable. Stand or sit on the floor.

2. Say "I want" out loud and pause ten to fifteen seconds, noticing what arises in your mind and body. Focus on the process. Notice if you have thoughts, images or sen-

sations in what parts of your body, and note the order of your process. Repeat "I want" and pause many times, until you have a sense of your process. Experiment with different inflections and intensities. For example, say "I want" in a whining voice, or ferociously, pleadingly or powerfully.

3. Say "I want" as you reach out to grasp something imaginary. Pause for ten to fifteen seconds and notice what responds in your mind and body. Repeat several times.

4. Imagine that something you enjoy is in front of you. Say "I want" as you reach out for it. Pause and be aware of your reaction. Now imagine that something you don't enjoy is in front of you. Say "I want" as you reach out for it. Pause and be aware of how that affects your mind and body.

5. Now think of an area of your life that you would like to open to more creative choice. Close your eyes and ask, "What do I want?" and pause ten to fifteen seconds, noticing the feelings that emerge in your mind and body. Repeat two or three times. Study the nature of your response to see if it resembles your internal reponse to what you know you like or dislike.

   Often we don't get an answer to "What do I want?"; we get process, and we need to follow it in the same way we follow process in Bodymind Centering.

6. Now focus on another area you'd like to explore, or rest for a moment and return to normal awareness.

Introducing and integrating the principles of manifestation is part of the work with each client, and it is woven throughout the daily web of our lives. We invite you to practice and enjoy creating new possibilities for greater aliveness and unity in your life.

The Short Form of the Basic Instructions

M A S S

NEWTONIAN *(money, jobs, cars, houses, etc.)*

1. *Figure out what you think you want*
2. *Let yourself become willing to clear any limiting feelings and beliefs that are in the way*
3. *Create a pattern in space (pictures, feelings, words, writing)*
4. *Let go of it, with the intention that it will come in the perfect way and time*
5. *Be prepared to correct and slip into:*

E N E R G Y

EINSTEINIAN *(relationships, emotional issues, subtle material)*

1. *Look closely at what you're getting*
2. *Love yourself for not liking it (if you don't like it)*
3. *Love it the way it is*
4. *Be willing to get the message or lesson from the way it is; check results for the purpose of seeing current vibration level and true intention*
5. *Keep expanding in love until it shifts and you're open to:*

S P A C E

THE THIRD WAY *(tends to draw the relationships and material things to you that support your highest evolution)*

1. *Let it be okay for you to be the source*
2. *Get as comfortable as you can be in space (as opposed to positions)*
3. *Keep opening verbally and nonverbally to what is (you won't know what it is if you're doing it right)*
4. *Affirm your commitment to your own and the universe's highest purpose*

The Energy Centers of the Body

In our work we look at the body both as a whole and as interlocking segments. Each segment, or zone, contains its own feelings and issues that emerge as work on that zone proceeds. The zones are eyes, throat/jaw/mouth, chest, diaphragm, abdomen and pelvis. After a general discussion of the concept of body centers, we will describe each zone separately.

In traditional Hindu psychology, the word *chakra* is used to denote a psychospiritual place in the body. This word, meaning *wheel* in Sanskrit, is very descriptive, especially if one looks at what nerve plexi look like. Each plexus has a core, or hub, with spokes radiating out from it. Two other Sanskrit words used to denote chakras are *granthi* (knots) and *sankhocha* (contraction). These terms show a remarkable understanding of what is actually going on in body centers. There are places which radiate energy, surrounded by knots and contractions caused by wounds and withdrawals. There are certain core places in the body which regulate and handle key issues, and around those places are the fundamental contractions that pattern our movements and the quality of the breathing cycle. The purpose of therapy is to undo the knots, so that the underlying positive energy can be expressed.

For example, a seven-year-old girl we worked with had a very contracted chest. It was sloped and caved in. With gentle movement therapy, a great deal of sadness was released. Her chest came out and up, and it emerged that she had always reached out to her father for love, but he rejected her because she reminded him too much of all the pain and anger he felt about her mother. The positive core impulse of love had been thwarted and had gone into hiding behind knots and contractions. By releasing the knots and bringing the issue out into the open, she was able to find new ways of dealing with it which did not cost her so much in tension in her body.

The Eye Zone

*T*he ocular zone, involving the eyes, forehead, ears and the back of the head, is a crucial segment for several reasons. Much tension accumulates here as a result of trying not to see painful things. Not seeing had survival value when we were children. Seeing what was actually going on around us would have overwhelmed us with pain. In addition, our seeing would have threatened the equilibrium of our families. We had to participate in the family trance to keep the family together. We have to move to see, and to not see we contract and tighten all the muscles of the neck and forehead as if we are wearing visors. People who have armor in the eye zone feel tension and pain there as energy rises in their bodies through movement or breathwork.

Often in breathwork, as energy begins to build in the person, there is much flickering of the eyelids. Along with flickering, there will often be twitching and itching of the eyes. These phenomena often indicate that there is conflict between the person's old beliefs and the new information that the brain is receiving from the energy building in the body. Why this should read out in the eye zone is not clear, unless it is because the eyes are the part of the body most directly connected to the brain.

Along with being "the windows of the soul," the eyes are also the window to the sensing of space. Being willing to see, the ocular equivalent to telling the truth, leads to increased awareness of internal space and increased fluidity in external movement patterns. Many times in breath and movement work, the person returns to that time in life when the eyes were contracted to avoid seeing pain.

The following examples are indicative of this phenomenon:

- averting the eyes to avoid seeing Daddy drunk again,
- not making eye contact because of having been punished for staring,
- learning a habit from Mom of looking away when angry.

A perceptual habit in the eye zone affects the entire body, even the way the feet contact the floor. For example, one man had retracted and narrowed the left side of his body. The left eye was also retracted and visibly less luminous than the right eye. When he explored these parts of his body, it emerged that he had retracted and hidden his feminine side during his life, as a way of keeping his feared homosexual feelings at bay. Even his left foot was turned slightly inward in comparison to the right foot.

Problems in the eye zone can manifest in numerous ways. Eyestrain is endemic in our culture. Much eyestrain is caused by reaching out with the eyes, rather than relaxing and letting information come to them. An image we frequently give clients is to let the eyes be windows rather than telescopes. The extreme extension of the problem is the head-forward, suspicious look of the paranoid. He is straining to scan the environment for threats which will never be found because they are all coming from behind the eyes. In some schizophrenics, there is such a pronounced left-right split that the eyes are two different colors.

For most of the population, though, the eye block revolves around trying not to see things that would mean pain. A woman efforts to avoid seeing her husband's affairs; to see the truth would mean the end of the marriage. A man develops headaches in the back of his head; they go away when he sees the truth of his difficult job situation. Sometimes it is much easier to deal with headaches than it is to change a job or a relationship. A glance at the afternoon soap operas is revealing. The commercials are more often from the makers of pain medications than from soap manufacturers.

The Mouth/Jaw/Throat Zone

*T*his zone, with its role in taking nourishment and in communication, is a major area of blocking in the body. If our oral needs go unsatisfied, we suck on costly substitutes such as cigarettes, chocolate and our fingernails. If our oral-aggressive feelings are not dealt with in a healthy manner, we store excessive amounts of tension in the jaw and throat. Once I (GH) was seated next to a well-known author and lecturer during a meeting in which several issues were being heatedly debated. I noticed that when she experienced flashes of anger, which happened about every other minute, she would clench her jaw, causing the muscles to bulge. After the meeting, she mentioned in conversation that she had just been to an orthodontist, who recommended $9000 worth of TMJ work to correct distortions of the jaw. It was obvious to me that the problem was a bad emotional habit rather than a dental issue. How many issues that we treat through medical intervention are actually psychological in nature? Estimates vary, ranging up into the neighborhood of 80 percent. There are hundreds of studies going on now to look into this rich area of potentially helpful knowledge.

This example points to an important aspect of the mouth/jaw/throat zone. Issues in other zones will have a correspondence in the oral zone. For example, a person may feel sad (a chest issue), and this sadness will be linked to tightening in the throat. This is because every time there is a hidden feeling there is a withheld communication. Every time a feeling is swallowed, armor is built up in the oral zone.

There are two major issues in this zone. The first is a receptive issue; the second is an expressive one. The first issue is whether or not we can get our needs for nourishment satisfied. This problem begins with physical nourishment, of course, but soon generalizes to other types of social, emotional and spiritual nourishment. Basically, then, armor in the oral zone is related to failing to get what we need at the deepest level, and what we want at a more superficial level.

The second issue in this zone is the armor caused by holding back expression. People have been punished for expression for a long time, from Galileo to Andrei Sakharov. On a more familiar level, people are punished in their families for all sorts of expression. Some of this expression is, of course, invalid, ineffectual and offensive. Children should be discouraged from swearing in church, farting at McDonalds, being rude or bullyish, etc. Unfortunately, much of what children are punished for is simply a matter of narcissistic whim on the part of parents.

It is interesting to note that in the tradition of Kundalini yoga the throat block is the key to the development of psychic powers. When this area opens and allows energy to move through, the adept supposedly has an increase in *siddhis* (supernormal powers). It is very clear from doing breathwork that the throat is the most important release center in the body. This observation may be due to several factors. First, the throat is the last area as we proceed downward over which we have much conscious control. You can consciously open your eyes, your jaw and your throat, but you cannot affect the chest and lower areas as much. Second, the role of communication in human life is paramount. The throat is exquisitely sensitive to constriction; the slightest holding back of expression shows up as tension in the zone. Third, birth trauma shows up in the throat, due to choking on fluids, having the cord wrapped around the neck and having the head and neck twisted by forceps. After being with many hundreds of people as they relived—and relieved—these ancient constrictions in the throat, we have come to have a deep appreciation of the throat's sensitivity.

Chest and Diaphragm

*A*nger and sadness are stored in the chest along with corollary issues such as rejection and longing. At the deeper levels in the chest, one encounters love and forgiveness. These positive emotions cannot be produced on cue; they are the result of clearing away the negative emotions that obscure them. In other words, the path to forgiveness of someone is often through giving yourself permission to feel anger and sadness at them. Then, the forgiveness is experienced spontaneously as a body event rather than a mental one.

A woman in her mid-fifties came in to work on depression. She had been given anti-depressants, which gave her some relief, but they made her feel "strange and out of touch with myself." She wanted to try to deal with the depression in a non-medical way. A glance at her chest revealed the problem. Her chest barely moved with inspiration, and there was no discernible movement on exhalation. It was concave from the top of her sternum down to her abdomen. We said, "It looks as if you have experienced a deep grief." This observation triggered deep sobbing, and her chest began to move with her breath. As she began to tell her story of death and loss, her chest stopped moving again. We encouraged her to stay with the feelings and leave the story for a while. She breathed into her chest and more sadness poured forth. After fifteen minutes of breathing and sobbing, she looked and felt like a different person. It turned out that she had never dealt with the death of her husband and mother, both of whom died within a short period of time. Medicated out of her depression, she had never felt it or breathed with the feelings beneath it. Over the next few weeks, we helped her open up to sadness and anger, while gently working with sore places on her back and chest, and underneath her collarbones. Finally she was able to breathe fully and freely in the chest without stirring up unclaimed emotions.

Breathing in the chest will stimulate emotional release in most people since most of us have some areas in which we have held on to feelings. The movement of the chest is directly connected to how deeply we can breathe, and how deeply we breathe is directly connected to whether we stop breathing to control feelings we do not want to feel. This phenomenon occurs in people from infants to octogenarians.

While it is possible to press on the tight muscles of the chest, one cannot push hard on the diaphragm. It does not respond to pressure, although it can be loosened from within by having the person cough and gag repeatedly. More often, though, the diaphragm begins to move when the person opens up to and releases the deeply held negative feelings in the chest. Often, as the diaphragm begins to move, one sees more explosive versions of the same emotions one encountered in the chest segment.

The diaphragm is the gateway to the deeply pleasurable feelings in the lower body. Anatomically, the diaphragm divides the body in half, separating the support functions of the lower body from the later-evolutionary expressive functions of the upper body. In the medieval European oral tradition, the diaphragm was considered the seat of the soul. As we work down the body, the diaphragm controls whether the person will begin to take pleasure in the breath. As the diaphragm loosens, the person will start to feel deeply pleasurable, breeze-like sensations with breathing. Reich called these "streamings," an excellent choice of words, as it describes the sensation accurately.

Optimum tonus of the diaphragm may be checked in the following way. Have the person take a deep breath, hold it, then rock the breath back and forth between abdomen and chest. If the armor is pronounced, the person will not be able to do it. If the armor is moderate, there will be difficulty and laboredness. If the diaphragm is relaxed and unarmored, the movement will be smooth and easy.

There are two major movement issues expressed through the chest and diaphragm centers. All the expressions of our arms originate in the chest and shoulder blade area: reaching out, giving and receiving, holding back power, anger or communication. Many emotional releases have been facilitated by asking clients to reach out into an imagined treasure chest and bring into their body that which they most want and need. Letting go and moving on emerge from an unblocked chest that has released sadness and anger. Choosing to reach out, risking contact and possible rejection, and defining personal space are dependent on opening the heart and backing it up with the power of the diaphragm.

Abdominal Zone

*T*he belly zone is the place where most people experience fear. This zone also allows us access to feelings of deep satisfaction and completion. Birth traumas may also be stored here since it is where we were cut off from the source. This area of the body becomes activated whenever we do not have an effective problem-solving strategy for a given situation. Often when people have just let go of a long-held belief, even though it might be ineffective, the belly zone is activated. They may feel waves of fear, even nausea.

Some of the fear issues that emerge when the belly zone is opening are failure, inadequacy, powerlessness, dying and going crazy. These fears must be completed by allowing ourselves to feel them fully. Fear cannot be catharted. We can discharge anger by pounding or sadness by crying. However, fear does not have a cathartic component. It must simply be felt fully and communicated verbally until it clears. Fear is the emotion of withdrawal. When we contract our awareness from something, the fear vibration begins. The solution is to expand again to embrace and feel the object of the original contraction. Dancing with these feelings quiets the vibration of fear.

The belly is the very center of the body and allows us to feel open to contact with the world. Incompleted fear makes energy rise in the body and takes us out of touch with the groundedness of being in touch with our center.

When breath moves in the abdomen, it usually stirs up old negative feelings. Once these are breathed through, there is a world of deeply positive feeling in this zone. This is the area in which we can feel deep relaxation, satisfaction, and a true sense of power. In addition, deep breathing in the abdomen is very healing for the abdominal organs. We have seen many cases of belly-level physical problems, such as colitis and ulcers, disappear as the person opened up to abdominal feelings and got energy moving in those areas again. An example of this type of healing may illustrate.

106

We had a client, a physician in his late thirties, who had a great deal of tension in his jaws and an ulcer. We loosened up the jaw tension and put him in touch with the anger held in this zone. After he spent several sessions working on anger issues, the ulcer flared up. As he opened up to the belly zone through breathing and verbally communicating his fears, the ulcer quieted down and eventually healed. With the increased energy and a sense of new-found power he experienced, he made a number of changes in his work and personal life.

Pelvic Zone

*T*he pelvic zone can be visualized by imagining a belt an inch or two above the pubic bone reaching around the back of the buttocks. This zone has three main issues in it.

The first major issue in the pelvic zone is the general attitude of holding back and withdrawing from life energy. If one is unwilling to fully participate in life, there will usually be retraction in the pelvis. The slang phrase to "get down" is quite descriptive, for if one is fully open to life energy the pelvis is down and forward. If one is holding back, the pelvis will be pulled up and back toward the spine.

A second major pelvic issue is resistance to one's deepest sexuality. This is closely related to the third issue: resistance to one's deepest anger. Both sexual feeling and anger are explosive feelings, and one of the major arts of living is to learn to contain explosive feelings without extinguishing them. The resistance to both these feelings is due to the fear of flying apart, of going crazy, of coming unglued. It is for this reason that it is wise to open armor from the top down, so that the person is gradually accustomed to higher and higher levels of energy before confronting the awesome energies of the pelvic zone.

Some of the main beliefs related to the pelvis are "I won't play (participate in life fully)" and "If I let myself feel my full anger and sexuality I'll fly apart." One thing that impedes people on spiritual paths is unwillingness to experience the rougher end of the vibrational spectrum. That is the reason it is ultimately futile for anyone to engage in spiritual practice who is not fully in touch with sexuality. To be fully evolved, consciousness must freely radiate in all directions. To numb out at one end of the body is to numb out all over.

Moshe Feldenkrais once said, "You are where your pelvis is." In other words, if the pelvis is held back, the whole being is held back. One's sense of being at home in the world is closely tied to one's ability to occupy the pelvis. Four-footed animals are much more at home on the earth than we are. The pelvis can be thought of as the fulcrum in the move to uprightness. And it is precisely the difficulty of dealing with our "animal" emotions, such as anger and sexuality, that causes problems in the pelvic zone. We have worked with countless people suffering from low back pain caused by retraction from anger and sexuality.

Movement in this area not only has to do with sexuality and participation with life, but also the survival issues of fight or flight. The legs and pelvis form a triangle of support that allows us to stand up for ourselves and stand on our own. A person who contracts and withdraws in the pelvis seems to be paralyzed between the two responses of fight or flight. Resolving pelvic issues creates dimensionality and fullness in the person's experience of aliveness. The pelvis is the center from which whole-body, or integrated, movement emerges.

It is also likely, though hard to prove, that brain function in general can be improved by increased freedom in the pelvis. The reason for this is that the movement of the cerebrospinal fluid, which originates in the brain, circulates down the spine and around the sacrum. We have seen many cases in which traumas to the pelvis have restricted the movement of the sacrum. When the restriction was released, the sacrum moved much more fluidly and the person reported increased alertness, concentration and other signs of improved brain function.

Summary

*T*he human being is made of interlocking segments, related to each other by function. The parts are a whole, but wholeness is impeded by stored emotional/psychological/spiritual issues in the particular zones. For spiritual evolution to proceed optimally, it is important to spot and deal with unfinished business in specific zones. For example, a long-time meditator and well-known channel came to us. She had headaches and a very collapsed chest. Over several sessions, she brought to light a lot of ancient anger and sadness. The chest came up and forward out of its old "give-up" position, and the headaches eased. Following these changes, her meditations became more rewarding and her channeling became more satisfying to her. There is no need to soar heavenward while dragging the body behind as a burden. It is easier, more fun, and ultimately more rewarding, to use the body itself as the medium for transcendence.

Centers of the Body

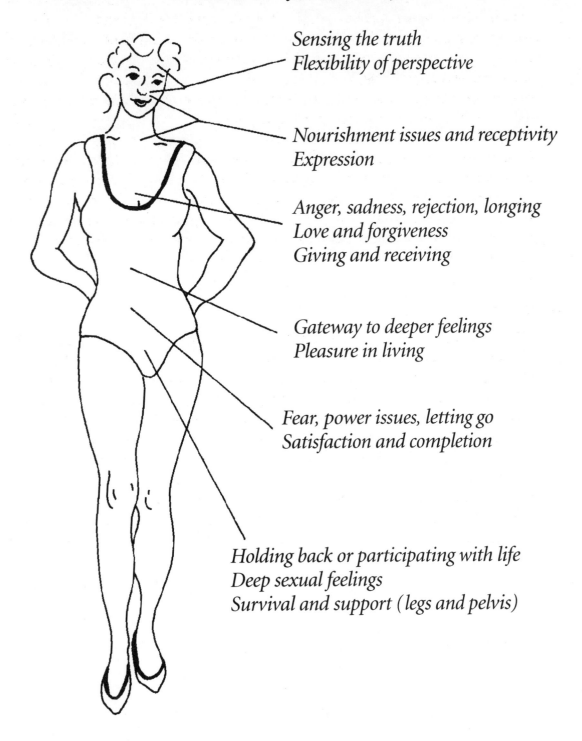

Sensing the truth
Flexibility of perspective

Nourishment issues and receptivity
Expression

Anger, sadness, rejection, longing
Love and forgiveness
Giving and receiving

Gateway to deeper feelings
Pleasure in living

Fear, power issues, letting go
Satisfaction and completion

Holding back or participating with life
Deep sexual feelings
Survival and support (legs and pelvis)

CHAPTER NINE

Frequently Asked Questions

*I*n this chapter we present the most frequently asked questions about bodywork, therapy and transformation in general. The questions are drawn from several sources. Some come from lectures and presentations before professional audiences. Others come from the students in our yearly certification programs in body therapy. Still others come in by mail or by phone from therapists around the world who are doing deeper experiential work. For us, a good question is one of the joys of life, and so we are grateful to all those who contributed the questions for this section.

1. *What is the purpose of bodywork and therapy?*

The purpose is to increase the amount of positive energy you can handle. Another way to say it is that the purpose is to heighten your ability to give and receive love. There are thousands of ways people keep themselves from experiencing positive energy: ruminating about the past, starting arguments, thinking of something else they have to do, needing to be right, injuring themselves, getting sick, etc. Therapy is about spotting all the ways you block positive energy and learning to let more through. Ultimately, if we let enough through, we become aware of our personal contact with universal energy, the divine.

2. *What advice have you found yourself giving most often over the years?*

Three things: Feel your feelings, tell the truth, keep your agreements. Practically all the problems for which people come to therapy involve a deficit in one or more of these areas. Of course, many people come from backgrounds in which they have been punished for telling the truth or opening up to certain feelings, so it's easy to see how they have fallen out of the habit. However, many people continue to avoid telling the truth or opening up to themselves because they are afraid of the pain. Keeping agreements is important, too, because it affects the quality of one's social relationships. For example, in every couple's-therapy session we've ever done, one or both people had a problem with broken agreements.

When we say to feel your feelings, tell the truth and keep your agreements, we aren't making a moral statement. The real issue is that these are all ways of increasing the amount of love and positive energy in your life. The failure to do these three things will severely limit the amount of positive energy that's available.

3. *Who is, and isn't, a candidate for breathwork?*

We generally don't recommend doing breathwork with psychotic or borderline individuals unless you have a support system that can assist them through the full unwinding process. These types of clients need to form stronger ego boundaries, whereas breathwork dissolves ego boundaries. Since breathwork takes the person into space, it is best used with people who have their feet fairly well on the ground. If in doubt, work with the person in movement which, since it is up in gravity, will not take the person quite so far out into space.

4. *During a breathwork session, how do I ask people to try a different breathing rhythm or style without making them think they're doing it wrong?*

One thing you can do is ask them if they would like a suggestion. If they say yes, make your intervention. As rapport builds with the person, it is less necessary to do this, but in the beginning it's not a bad idea to ask first.

If the person is pushing really hard we will usually suggest that they lighten up. If they are hardly breathing, we will suggest that they pick up the pace and intensity. Otherwise we tend to let the breath do the work.

5. *What is tetany, and what should I do when a person goes into it during a session?*

Tetany can occur for several reasons. It often happens when the rising energy of the breathwork comes up against a long-held block. For example, it often signals the emergence of birth trauma. Sometimes it is simply because the person is taking a fuller out-breath than in-breath. Ask the person to deepen the in-breath and relax the out-breath. If the tetany has been caused by pushing the out-breath, it will usually clear up. However, if there is birth trauma or some deeply-held feeling beneath the tetany, encourage the person to relax into it and feel what is beneath it.

The length of time tetany will stay depends entirely on the person's belief system. We have seen it clear up within seconds when the person became willing to feel what was beneath it. If the person's belief system is that tetany is bad, it will stay around for a long time. One rebirther said that an obstetrician he was rebirthing stayed in tetany for five hours, because the doctor had such a strong belief system that tetany was a medical problem.

6. *When I do not know what to do next with a client, either in breathwork or in movement therapy, what is the best thing to do?*

Go into your own body. Tune in to your breath, your movement, and your body sensations. Oscillate your attention between noticing your inner experience and tuning in to the client. Stay with it until something emerges. Encourage your client to do the same. Invite the person to experience bodily sensations, feel where the breath is and isn't going, deepen the breath. It's wise to trust the cellular wisdom of the body and what it needs to do next.

Not knowing what to do can be a useful state to explore.

7. *What is the meaning of extreme shifts in body temperature during breathwork? My body gets cold, then hot, and often begins involuntarily shaking and vibrating.*

The vibrations signal that tension is being released from the body and are valuable signs that the breath is getting into places that haven't awakened. Cold usually indicates some old fear is releasing or that birth trauma is being accessed. Heat is usually a sign that the energy has penetrated a previously blocked zone. Stay with the process, if possible, until the temperature has stabilized.

8. *If the client begins making sounds during breathwork or movement, should I encourage it?*

Encourage the person to go all the way with the sound. The best energy sensations are beneath all sounds, but the person often has to make sounds for a while in order to get there. They will get to the deepest energy spaces if they move through the sounds quickly. It is not effective for the person to grind away on one particular sound for a long time. People usually do this to resist going deeper. You will recognize this type of sound because it has a grating quality to it. Encourage them to go all the way with it, make it more intense, or get beneath it to the pure breath or movement that wants to emerge.

9. *How much intellectualizing and verbalizing are appropriate at the end of a session?*

We usually tell people to stay with their bodily experience as long as they can, and let the intellectual awarenesses come organically later. It is best if people are grounded and still in their bodies after a session, rather than up in their minds. We tend to encourage walking, gentle moving about, rather than analyzing immediately after a session.

10. *I often question how much I should intervene during breathwork or movement. Is there a formula?*

In general, the less the better. Much of our work is based on the person going within, tuning in to what's there, and letting it turn into breath or movement. At its best, the work proceeds organically, with the person finding the next direction from his or her own internal process. Often the best sessions are those in which the interventions are purely on the telepathic level, with little touch or verbal interaction.

113

11. *What about clients who go to sleep during breathwork? Should I wake them or let them wake themselves up?*

Some people go to sleep as a defense against the rising energy. Others go to sleep because they are flushing anesthesia out of the system, either from birth or from surgery. After you have identified that it is a pattern and have pointed this out, ask the person if he or she would prefer to be kept awake, awakened by you, or allowed to come out of the sleep organically. The person may even wish to try it several different ways. We have seen people go to sleep dozens of times before finally breaking through the pattern. When people want to breathe through the sleepiness, have them take rapid breaths just as they are feeling the first edge of the sleepiness.

12. *What question do you find yourself asking clients more than any other?*

What sensations are you experiencing in your body right now? This question homes the person in on the body very quickly. Once the contact with the body sensations is established, magic can happen.

13. *How much should I tell a person about the process of breathwork or movement before he or she experiences it?*

We like to send a prospective client a written description of the basic techniques we use prior to the first session. We have found that this practice cuts down on the amount of time necessary for explanation. If this is not possible, then give the person enough explanation so that he or she feels comfortable. People who have a lot of questions about bodywork are usually experiencing fear. In this case, discuss the fear rather than loading them up with more information.

14. *Do you give homework between sessions?*

Yes. Any one of several things may be asked of the person: breathwork, movement, Bodymind Centering, acupressure. Occasionally with headache clients we give them a portable biofeedback device to use at home. Sometimes other homework is tailored to the individual. Among these activities are journal-keeping, artwork, long walks and meditation. With certain clients, particularly those with low energy and little armor, joining a health club is prescribed.

15. *What if the person goes through an hour or so of breathing with no emotional release, birth material or anything else coming up? Just positive feelings, like bliss, energy, etc.?*

Wonderful! If there are no blocks in the way that day, or in general, there will be simply a deep experience of bliss and positive energy. Earlier we said that the purpose of therapy is the expansion of positive energy and the ability to give and receive love. There is no reason to mess with one's pain other than to move through it to more love.

16. *Once I had a client express an intention that he was willing to let go of all the rage in his life. Following this, he experienced more rage than ever. He got calls from an angry ex-wife who hadn't spoken to him in years, a car backed into his car in a parking lot, and several other things happened which brought up rage. Is this typical?*

There is nothing like expressing a clear, positive intention to flush all the unfinished business out of your life. It sounds like the intention opened the floodgates that allowed him to see clearly where his anger was attached. Once a man called us from another state to ask our advice about birth trauma. The man suspected he was carrying around a lot of it. He told us he was willing to do anything to clear it up. We recommended a therapist in the man's area, and he went to see our colleague that day. The next morning at 5 AM we got a call from the man, who said he had been up all night breathing out anesthesia. "You didn't tell me about this part of it," he said, not unpleasantly. We reminded him of the intention he had expressed, just the day before, that he would do anything to clear out his birth trauma. "Yes," he said, "but I didn't know it was going to cost me sleep!"

A lot of us are like that. We want to wake up, but not if it is going to disturb our sleep. It is important, particularly when you express a clear intention such as, "I want to wake up," that you are willing to ride out whatever needs to happen to make the intention realized.

One suggestion we often make to clients is to express the intention in a safe way. For example, one can think, "I want to clear up my birth trauma in a way that's friendly to myself and others." This phrasing expresses the intention more specifically. As another example, a friend of ours wanted to go on a meditation retreat in Switzerland, but he didn't have the thousand dollars for it and he couldn't sell his car. He was overheard to say that he would do anything to get to the retreat. Later in the week he was rear-ended by another driver, which got rid of our friend's car problem. It was totalled. His settlement was a little over a thousand dollars. Now, this is one way to get what you want, but he could also have been hurt. It is wise to express the intention with care, so that when the universe fills your order, you get exactly what you want in the way you want it.

17. *What attitude do you think could best serve people in their lives and in their work on themselves?*

An attitude of genuine inquiry. By this we mean that people could bring to life an intention to learn about their life processes simply for their own sake. So many people get trapped by an intention to be right, or to control others, or to prove that the world doesn't really work, or one of the thousands of other intentions that limit effectiveness. Life frees up a great deal when the intention is purely to inquire into things with no other gain expected, as if the inquiry itself is reward enough.

18. *What are the main differences between Radiance Breathwork and other forms such as rebirthing, pranayama and Grof breathwork?*

    We've been asked this question often, and we've often replied that comparing personal growth techniques is a little like comparing lovers: rarely useful and potentially tacky. Several distinctions can be made, however. Radiance Breathwork is not focused on the birth event, although birth experiences are welcome should they occur. We take a more open-ended approach, studying carefully the individual's particular breathing style. Many rebirthers also emphasize complex belief systems about physical immortality and other speculative things, while we say that one of the main goals of Radiance Breathwork is to get beyond belief systems. Our graduates spend nine months with us, whereas there are less standardized training procedures for other forms of breathwork.

    With regard to pranayama, there are so many hundreds of different techniques that you could probably find one that resembles just about any form of contemporary breathwork. The ancient Indian masters were great geniuses at developing techniques, and although our techniques are not derived from pranayama, we have great respect for the systems with which we have had contact. People have told us that the work developed by Stan Grof, with his extensive background in psychedelic drugs, is somewhat similar to ours, although the Grof sessions are usually longer (two to three hours) and conducted in groups. Many of our sessions are conducted in groups, but we also train our graduates how to do individual breathwork in their private practices. Our sessions are shorter (usually one to two hours), because we feel that longer sessions can bring up more than the person can comfortably integrate afterwards.

    Also, unlike many other forms of breathwork, ours places a great deal of emphasis on grounding, expression and integration into life. As we've often said, it's very easy to get someone high during breathwork, but it requires much more skill and care to orchestrate an experience that one can integrate into life. Our suggestion is to try out several different systems and see which one you like best.

19. *Can you say something about how symptoms (e.g., headaches, fears, relationship issues) clear up in the work?*

    Symptoms are usually ways the person has developed to deal with the underlying energy. For example, somebody may use headaches to deal with the underlying energy of anger. When the energy is dealt with directly, the symptom is no longer needed. Interestingly, we have noticed over the years that clients who clear up symptoms often do not report their success right away. The report is usually prefaced by, "Oh, by the way," as in, "Oh, by the way, I haven't had a headache for the last few weeks." It's as if they often forget that they had the symptom. We have observed this phenomenon even with difficult problems such as cancer.

20. *What can I do to encourage movement in people who normally feel uncomfortable in their bodies?*

This is a very common situation for 20th century bodies. When the purpose of the work is to focus on experiencing the body, people can become very self-conscious and feel as if they are performing and being judged. There are several ways to encourage more ease in movement exploration: Share your experience in your body when you move; bring their awareness to gestures and postures that occur as they speak; explore HOW they make themselves uncomfortable; use Kinetic Bodymind Centering with an emphasis on tense areas; bring their awareness to their breath as they move in everyday ways, such as walking, starting and stopping, getting larger and smaller, etc.; have them ask their body what is needed to begin to feel comfortable (e.g., eyes closed, not having to do anything). We often start movement with new clients by exploring all the ways we can make ourselves self-conscious, then we can continue relating as equals without that social sense of separation.

21. *How do I know what to focus on in movement therapy among all the gestures and motions?*

There will be some sense of "charge" around important movements, ones that can lead the mover deeper into his or her experience. The mover will emphasize them in some way, either by repetition, tone and intensity of voice, breath holding, or other nonverbal highlighting. The movement will also appear unintegrated. In other words, the impulse won't flow congruently through the body, but will appear separate in some way. The mover can also signal an important area by attempting to hide that part of themselves (e.g., slumping shoulders, restrained finger flicking, etc.). Probably the best way to sense what is important is to pay attention to and trust your own body responses.

22. *What is the most useful intention for the therapist to hold in the work?*

We as therapists have the opportunity to hold the space for clients to be complete. Perhaps the most useful intention for us to hold, then, is that it is all right for the client to go all the way. To do this, however, we need to hold this intention for ourselves. We need to know in our cells that it is all right to go down through the many layers of ourselves to behold and experience the power of pure awareness. We need to know cellularly that at the bottom of all experience is the divine. If we can provide the space for our clients to open to everything they are, to feel all their feelings and be conscious of what they have always resisted, and if we know that by doing so they will uncover their fundamental divinity, then we are holding the correct intention for the work to proceed.

CHAPTER TEN

Aphorisms and Notes on Therapy and Transformation

The following material is gathered from tapes and written notes taken by students during spontaneous interchanges at trainings, workshops and private meetings. Unless otherwise noted, Gay is the speaker.

We get exactly the experience we need to be having. It is either a new lesson we need to learn, or a coming-around-again of something we missed learning before. Our problem begins when we think "This isn't the experience I'm supposed to be having." We withdraw and set up a duality. The only solution is to see each experience as exactly what ought to be happening. Then we can do something creative about it.

We are made up of a bunch of stuff (personality, meat, ideas) wrapped around a system of energy. The energy is permeated by space. Energy and space are also all around us. For example, if you look closely at the leaves of a tree or the skin of a human being, you can see energy radiating out a few inches into space. So, we have energy and space, and it has us.

Energy by its very nature is a dancer. It wants to create, celebrate. Part of us wants to dance with the energy and part of us is afraid of it. The part of us that resists the dance of energy does so because in the past we got in trouble for dancing with it. We opened up to it, and something bad happened. Now we may have a belief that says "If I open up to more energy, life and love I will experience pain." So we keep the volume turned way down.

In addition, we have a stack of old messages from parents, churches and other sources that tells us it is wrong/sinful/harmful to open up to our own creative energy. Plus, we are all afraid of the unknown, and to jump out into energy and space is to take a giant leap into the unknown. We want to make a deal: I'll get somebody else to experience it, and if they turn out okay then I'll give it a try.

We need to learn in our cells that energy always feels good. Resisting it is what feels bad. If we resist it we feel tense, stuck, sick, like we're having no fun. Sometimes when we're about to make a breakthrough, the conflict between the part of us that wants to open up and the part that wants to stay shut feels awful. That's when we need friends who can tell us: Go ahead, open up, feel the truth, acknowledge what is. What is inside us already is. Opening up to it doesn't make it worse; staying shut to it doesn't make it go away.

Everybody gets stuck now and then. Life is not about trying to avoid being stuck, though some of us spend a lot of time and energy doing just that. Life is about the process of getting stuck and unstuck. Some of us stay stuck nearly constantly; the reason is that we are trying desperately to avoid being stuck. A good measure of progress in life is how often we get stuck and unstuck, and how many ways we know how to get unstuck. Being stuck is usually about slowing down because we need to learn or experience something. What frees us is being willing to look at or experience the truth. Most times we won't know what the truth is until we get willing to experience it.

Here are some of my favorite ways of getting unstuck:

Adjust the mind to be willing to feel. Slow down if you're going too fast. Tell the truth, starting with what nobody could argue with. For example, start talking, saying things like "I'm standing up right now, I'm wearing a blue sweater, I see some snow outside." Then progress to more subtle things like "I'm feeling scared, I'm confused . . ." Listen. Breathe. Move. Love.

Every feeling, if we fully experience it, leads to unity, bliss and God-consciousness. We really have to learn this notion in our bodies. Next time you are feeling angry or sad, breathe into it, opening up to it, staying with it through its changes. Keep breathing and moving with it, and you will soon notice that it turns into pure energy. Stay with the energy and it will eventually turn into space. Stay with space and you will learn something about God.

The short path requires that we drop linear notions of how the world works. One linear notion that many of us have tattooed on our souls is that we have to go back and forth between happy and sad, fun and crash, pleasure and pain, good times and bad times. We get close to a loved one, then quick as a wink we're in an argument. Let's trade in that old linear programming for a new way of being: Life is an

120

expanding opportunity to feel more and more positive energy. Instead of have fun/have a crash, let's re-program ourselves to have fun/take a rest, have more fun/take a rest. The notion that bad has to follow good is simply a belief.

In space there is no time. In time there's no space. When we're in time there is a certain pain intrinsic to it. When we're in pain we need to go into it, to experience it deeply enough to find the space in it.

Problems are often created by our trying to have the solution fit our preconceived notions of how things ought to be. This is particularly true with our spiritual problems. Since we don't know best how to know God, all we can do is express the intention and stand back to experience it.

Person at workshop: If I really open up to my sadness, won't I feel depressed and never get out of it?
Gay: No, that's a belief. We believe that if we open up to our sexuality we'll become rampant. If we open up to our anger we'll kill somebody. That's the voice of our ego, trying to keep us in the boundary of the known. Go ahead and feel the feeling to completion. You'll find that there's nothing at the bottom of our feelings but bliss and space. Inappropriate acting-out comes from *not* letting ourselves feel.

Person at workshop: Is there a light at the end of the tunnel?
Gay: There's probably a tunnel at the end of all this light.

Person at workshop: How do I get rid of this anger I feel?
Gay: It's probably not a good idea to think of getting rid of anything. What we want to do is open up, feel it deeply. As you do that a space opens up around it. Picture your anger as a wild bull in your backyard. Rather than going out and beating him out of the yard, build a huge pasture for him to run in. Then you can use the wild-bull energy but have it in perspective.

Question at lecture: How do I get through a creative block?
Answer: Whatever's there stays there until you love it. Love yourself for having the block.
Questioner: What if I don't know how?
Answer: That's the best place to start. Just love yourself for not knowing how.

You don't have to go around feeling all your feelings. That would be pretty noisy. You just have to be willing to feel them.

121

When we open to face pain and feel it completely, a space opens which holds both pain and happiness. This is what I think God is.

We set up extreme situations so there will be no way out but through. Trouble is, we often decide not to go through at the last moment, so we have to set up an even more extreme situation next time.

The source is not out there. I have experienced this at a level I cannot escape.

People are so much more interesting as who they are than who we want/wish/expect them to be.

There are two conditions: bliss and lessons to be learned.

Gratitude is the expression of a healed heart.

Miracles come in the space between beliefs, not as a reward for having lots of beliefs. It's important to be willing to float free in the place of no beliefs.

Breathing is so important because it's associated with that first moment, our first take on life. We went from unity to separateness in that moment. Was our first breath a celebration of autonomy or a deep experience of pain? Take a few deep breaths and you'll find out. If your breathing takes you directly to bliss, you had a good start at birth. If you're like most of us, you have to breathe through a gate of pain in order to recapture your birthright of bliss.

Confusion is a transition state between matter and space. Open up to it, celebrate it rather than resisting it. You have to go through a meltdown, a period of mushmind, to get into space.

Peace is total participation.

Reason has its limits. It can get us to the 7-11, but it can't get us to the light.

Power is how much space you are willing to occupy. The power in a situation always flows to the person who occupies the most space.

Symptoms are a form of expression, perhaps a crude way, perhaps an eloquent way of saying something that needs to be said. They are to be listened to, not just eliminated.

At the moment we express ourselves fully there is no fear. Fear only comes on the in-breath or on an incomplete out-breath. You may be afraid on the diving board, but at the moment of full expression—the dive—there is no fear.

Person at workshop: When do we become responsible for what happens to us?
Gay: Responsibility doesn't begin until the moment you take it. Before that, we are just as un-responsible as the two-year-old whose father comes home drunk and kicks her. There's no need to go back to the past and try to figure out if you created a situation. The two-year-old doesn't need to speculate later about whether she kicked her father in a past life. Just take responsibility NOW! Everything else is just a slow-down, a detour.

Willingness lines us up with what is, and puts the space between everything. Willingness is the transition place between matter and energy, energy and space.

There's a higher energy available right now. All we have to do is sleep a little less, feel a little more, love as much as we can.

The quality of vibration we experience inside is determined by how much energy and love we are willing to let through. Resistance roughens the vibrations.

Intention is the first framing of energy as it moves out of space. This is the best place from which to influence the material plane. We need to make sure we inquire into our unconscious intentions while making more conscious ones.

In a relationship you don't have to provide everything the other person needs. You just need to create a space for the person to get what he or she needs.

Telling the truth is the strongest aphrodisiac on earth.

Available from The Hendricks Institute:

Books

- **Conscious Loving: The Journey to Co-Commitment.** This pioneering book explores the commitments that transform co-dependence to conscious loving, the major traps of unconscious loving, the transformative power of the microscopic truth, and the one problem that needs to be solved. **Conscious Loving** includes a specific set of activities to put these ideas into daily use. Hardcover. $19.95
- **Centering and the Art of Intimacy.** Gay and Kathlyn's first breakthrough book on creating enlightening relationships contains chapters on getting close and separate, projection, and communications skills $6.95
- **Learning to Love Yourself.** Gay's bestselling book on the gentle art of loving your feelings, body, sexuality and Self is a beautifully written and effective guide to truly loving yourself. $7.95
- **The Learning to Love Yourself Workbook.** A hands-on guide to applying the lessons of Gay's **Learning to Love Yourself** in daily life $8.95

Audio tapes

- **The Art of Breathing and Centering.** Gay's new tape from Audio Renaissance contains four of his most powerful, non-threatening, easy to follow, and rapidly effective breathing activities, an explanation of why and how breathwork can be useful in personal evolution, and an accompanying booklet $9.95
- **The Healing Dialogue.** Kathlyn's voice leads you gently through a precise, step-by-step bodymind integration technique for solving life problems through contact with the Inner Self. Side One is designed to be experienced while sitting, and Side Two, The Kinetic Healing Dialogue, acknowledges the resources and information of your moving body $9.95
- **Radiance Breathing Meditation.** Gay's voice guides this breathing meditation, which is designed to be used daily to reset your body's energy thermostat at a higher level and expand your ability to experience positive energy. Side Two guides you through the Couples' Co-Meditation Process, designed to develop a sense of connection and feeling of harmony in relationship. $9.95

Videotapes

- **At the Speed of Love.** An hour-long, VHS-format video, features Gay Hendricks, Ph.D., and Kathlyn Hendricks, Ph.D., ADTR, a husband-wife team of psychologists, working with two individuals. Combining breathwork, movement therapy and process interventions, Gay and Kathlyn first work with Cyndy, whose initial relationship issue unfolds to the resolution of past sexual trauma. The subsequent session with her husband Ron illustrates several interventions for dealing with repressed feelings, birth trauma, and chronic physical tensions. Gay and Kathlyn discuss the major principles of their work, which The Hendricks Institute teaches in seminars for mental health professionals throughout the U.S. and abroad.... $35.00
- **Conscious Loving.** This hour-long, VHS-format video features Gay and Kathlyn at a recent Conscious Loving seminar. They present the key ideas and examples from their new book in a clear and entertaining exchange, including the Six Co-Commitments, the Nine Traps of Unconscious Loving, projection, and conscious communication $45.00

The Self-Healing Series

This set of four large, two-sided, laminated sheets presents a sequence of activities designed to enhance bodymind integration for specific problems.

- **Freedom from Asthma in 10 Minutes a Day** contains beginning and advanced breathing activities to release the diaphragm and open effective breathing.
- **Healing Migraine and Tension Headaches** presents preventive and headache release activities for dealing with this problem in a new way.
- **Healing Your Back Pain** is a daily program of ten bodywork, acupressure, breathwork and awareness activities.
- **Acupressure Relief** presents simple activities for dealing with common problems, such as headaches, indigestion, menstrual cramps, low back pain, stress, hiccups and acne .... $6.95 each, or $25.00 for the set

To order: Colorado residents add 6½% tax to your order. Please include $2.50 postage and handling for the first item and $1.50 for each additional item. Make checks payable to The Hendricks Institute. Visa or Mastercard orders ($15 or more), call: 1 (800) 688-0772. Address for ordering by mail or requesting information on Hendricks Institute courses: The Hendricks Institute, P.O. Box 994, Colorado Springs, Colorado 80901.